PROJECT MANAGEMENT
FOR EDUCATION

THE BRIDGE TO 21ST CENTURY LEARNING

Project Learning Guide for Project Managers

By Walter Ginevri and Bernie Trilling

D1551168

Library of Congress Cataloging-in-Publication Data has been applied for.

ISBN: 978-1-62825-457-0

Published by: Project Management Institute, Inc.
                14 Campus Boulevard
                Newtown Square, Pennsylvania 19073-3299 USA
                Phone: +1-610-356-4600
                Fax: +610-356-4647
                Email: customercare@pmi.org
                Internet: www.PMI.org

Book cover designed by: Andrea Staricco

All proceeds from the book will go to the PMI Educational Foundation, the authors have graciously agreed to forgo any royalties.

Table of Contents

Project Manager Foreword

by Jim Snyder, PMI Founder & Lifetime Innovator

As one of the founders of the Project Management Institute (PMI) back in the 1960s, I have long held a strong opinion that the only way for project management to reach its full potential in driving solutions to world problems was to create a generation of project-oriented people to solve project-oriented problems. The only way to achieve that objective would be to fully integrate project management skills into our K–12 educational programs. That means we must first have project-oriented educators—and this might be just a small problem! After all, business/industry and education are two very different worlds.

Project management is not rocket science, although there might not have been any rocket science without it! Project management—all that "stuff" that goes into the successful planning, organizing, executing, and delivery of successful project-oriented work—has become part of our everyday lives, and we acquire these skills in a very different way from most of our other life skills.

Like it or not, we have evolved to the point where most of our productive work takes the form of a project. Life is a series of continuing, overlapping, and interrelated projects. "Projects" are the way we get things done. Unlike many other skills, managing these various projects is important to our professional, social, and daily lives. The way we manage projects is not so very different from one environment to another, but we may acquire the skills we need to manage projects from very different sources.

Many of us had our first introduction to the world of project management in our professional lives when we found ourselves responsible for a major project. For many, it was an unexpected career change! We needed to learn quickly how to handle ourselves in the ever-changing and ever more complex world of projects. Our learning and knowledge base grew from our experiences in engineering, heavy construction, pharmaceuticals, aerospace, the military, and the oil and gas industries. The industrial acceptance and implementation of project management principles and practices soon spread to an ever-widening group of businesses and industries. Today, project management is a part of almost everything we do.

From the original industrial/business base, PMI developed *A Guide to the Project Management Body of Knowledge (PMBOK® Guide)*, which set the language for engineering and business project management. And now, providers of project management training, education, and consulting are available, worldwide, to the engineering and business communities based on the language, processes, and practices that have developed from the early 1960s. This has become the language of professional project management.

But what about those other environments, such as education, our social lives, and our daily activities in which managing project-oriented work is just as important? A 2006 report by the Partnership for 21ˢᵗ Century Skills found the U.S. workforce "ill-prepared for the demands of today's (and tomorrow's) workplace." Lacking were both basic skills and applied skills such as critical thinking, problem solving, oral communications, teamwork, leadership, and others—all components of the project management process. Studies like this one and others focused educators' attention on project based learning (PBL), developed by the Buck Institute for Education and many others. PBL is a teaching method that engages students in learning through participation in interdisciplinary projects. As the process and implementation of PBL continued to grow and became accepted by more and more educators in the late 1990s, it took on a language of its own.

Civic and community organizations, as well as governmental groups, have begun to use project management processes to meet the demands of 21ˢᵗ century project-oriented work. Project based learning educational programs are starting to reach into classrooms far down through the K–12 structure, universities are making project management courses of study from the Bachelor to PhD levels available to students of all ages, and industrial/business segments such as information technology are requiring project management skills, including agile project management training, for their professionals. With the explosion of interest and the application of new processes to manage project-oriented work, it was inevitable that the two project-related cultures would eventually meet. And now they have.

If it looks like a project, acts like a project, and has all the characteristics of a project, then it must be a project! If we manage it like a project, does it really matter what we call the processes we use? But the differences are not all in the language alone. Educators take a different approach to problem definition from that which might be taken by an engineer. There is little difference in the processes used by both communities; however, the emphasis and definition of these processes varies in the two communities. Confusions arise when the engineer and the educator try to collaborate on a research project or when a new business-oriented project manager joins an educational project team well-versed in PBL learning methods. Misunderstandings often result, reducing the efficiency and the effectiveness of the project teams. If only there were a way for these two communities to share their processes and learning without the possibility of confusion or misunderstandings.

In 2006 and 2007, the two communities made an effort to agree on common terminology and to bring their project processes together in a more unified approach. Some progress was made. However, no lasting agreements or translations from business to education terminology were fully developed. During the past few years, both the approaches to managing project-oriented work based in the professional (business/industrial) world and in the educational system have grown and matured.

The language and process differences between the way project-oriented work is understood in the world of business and in the world of education have continued to be ironed out. An understanding of the differences between these two worlds has become more important as managing projects becomes a true learning and life skill that impacts every aspect of our personal, social, and professional lives.

In the early days of project management, our concerns were to establish the processes and create a knowledge base for a new profession. And over the years, we have done that. However, it is no longer acceptable for the profession to rely on on-the-job learning as the major educational source for those undertaking responsibility for major projects. Future project managers must come to the job with the tools and skills they need. This can only be accomplished if project management becomes a major life skill taught as one of the basic tools needed to manage the projects of learning, work, and life. I believe the teaching of the basic and applied skills identified by the Partnership for 21st Century Skills back in 2006 must become a reality if we hope to meet the challenges of this century. Some progress has been made, but until we have fully integrated project management and project based learning into the K–12 curriculum, the job will not be done. Giving project managers and educators a better understanding of each other's viewpoints will go a long way toward making this needed integration a reality.

Walter Ginevri and Bernie Trilling have unique talents that allow them to address the issues of process and language differences that exist between project management and education. They both have experience in the world of education and in the world of business project management, and they have been acutely aware of the need for bringing the two worlds together for many years. This book aims to bridge these language and cultural barriers and empower both project management professionals and educators with the skills they need to bring their combined talents to bear on 21st century challenges.

The unique "flip" format of the book allows a quick change in perspective from educator to project manager and highlights the similarities as well as the differences in project processes and terminology. I think you will find this book a great step forward in support of the evolving transformation of education to meet our global, local, and business/education challenges. Use it to broaden your understanding of the management of life's projects: professional, business, social, or educational. Most of all, have some fun while learning to value and learn from the viewpoints of others—a much needed collaborative skill that will no doubt lead to a better world through all our learning, work and life projects to come!

James R. Snyder
Founder
Project Management Institute

Project Manager Preface

A "Two-Books-in-One" Overview

The book you are holding, *Project Management for Education ("PM4Ed"* for short)*, is actually two books in one: a *Project Manager Guide* and an *Educator Guide* to bringing the benefits of the powerful, practical principles and practices of project management to the world of education.

By flipping this book over, you can switch between the two guides to explore how both project managers and educators are increasingly striving toward the same goal—to help all students become more successful 21st century learners, well prepared for future work, citizenship, family, and community life.

PM4Ed aims to help build indispensable bridges between project management and education, to support the evolving transformation of education to equip all students with the essential skills to help tackle our world's "glocal" (global and local) problems, and to empower all learners to successfully manage their personal, social, and life challenges.

The *Project Learning Guide for Project Managers* (the side of the book you are now reading) offers a concise roadmap for adapting business-related project management expertise to the learning needs of teachers and students, bringing the power of project methods to education and empowering student learning projects around the globe.

It is presented in seven Project Manager Chapters:

1. Bringing Project Management to Schools, Educators, and Students
2. Project Management as Learning, Work, and Life Skills
3. School Projects Versus Business Projects
4. Project Management and Time Management
5. Agile and Adaptive Project Management
6. Educators as Project Managers
7. The Future of Project Management in Education

This is followed by the center rainbow-colored "bridge" section of the book (shared by both the *Project Manager* and *Educator* guides),

Project Bridges to 21ˢᵗ Century Learning, a series of illustrated examples of real-life learning projects carried out in primary through secondary classrooms and communities around the world. These authentic case studies of successful learning projects highlight the 21ˢᵗ century competencies students developed and the project learning strategies they used. They also demonstrate how professional project managers and educators can work together to help all students and teachers become more powerful project learners and leaders.

Also in this center bridge section is the Project Learning Resources materials, which offer a wide variety of supporting resources and tools for both project managers (PMs) and educators including project learning pathways, a project learning research summary, a 21ˢᵗ century skills framework description, a learning project methods comparison table, a project management for education glossary, lists of helpful books, online resources, and more.

If you flip the book over, you will be able to explore the *Project Learning Guide for Educators*, which introduces education-friendly versions of the tried-and-true success strategies that expert project managers have refined over lifetimes of practice and research.

With the support of the Project Management Institute Educational Foundation (PMIEF), project management principles and practices throughout both guides have been "translated" from the technical language of business and engineering and adapted to fit the common vocabularies of teachers and students working on learning projects in everyday classrooms.

Project Manager Author Page

Walter Ginevri

If I have seen further than others,
it is by standing upon the shoulders of giants.
—Isaac Newton

In 2006 I met Carlo Notari, president of the Project Management Institute's (PMI's) Northern Italy Chapter, a generous and passionate Southern Italian. As a typical Northern Italian—efficient, process driven, and anchored to reality—I was new to my position as the chapter's vice president of education and a little unsure of how we two project managers from such diverse backgrounds would work together.

It turned out there was absolutely no need to worry—our professional collaboration rapidly turned into a deep friendship, from the moment Carlo announced his dream to bring project management to the world of education through these words:

> *Our mission must not be limited to the members of a professional community, but also to the society we belong to. This means it's our duty to spread the project culture starting from the school and, since I know that your wife, Mariù, is a primary school teacher, you are the right person in the right place to make this happen.*

I remember that moment very well—though I had more doubts than certainties about applying project management to schools, especially for very young students, ages 6 to 11, I was thrilled by the prospects of helping to raise a new generation of students with the skills I knew were so important to their success in learning, work, and life.

As a "Socratic" project manager, very aware of doubts as necessary steps on the way to finding good solutions, I accepted the challenge and, thanks to Mariù and a team of highly motivated teachers, the first pilot projects were launched within three primary schools in Milan—two public and one private. The results of applying project principles and practices to student projects were surprisingly highly effective, and much of the success of these "early win" projects must be attributed to the teachers and the wise choices and careful attention given to their students.

First of all, the choice of developing an original approach to supporting young students in their project work, instead of adapting or simplifying methods used in the business context, made a huge difference. Second, the choice of preserving and amplifying the key role of the teacher by involving project management experts as coaches and advisors to teachers and their students as needed, was also an important step. Last but not least, the choice of adopting a set of visual tools well known in the school context, such as visual brainstorming and mind mapping, to maximize the transparency and flexibility of the project approaches and methods, was truly a key to our success.

I remember, during the early period of experimentation and learning, an interaction that provided proof that we were on the right path. A 10-year-old student named Ludovica, after completing a project building a puppet theater and putting on plays based on students' favorite fairy tales, summarized the most important impact of all the learning project work with a sentence that I'll never forget. She said:

> *Even the shiest children felt involved and took part in the teamwork.*

Can you imagine a better message to highlight the benefits of a project approach to learning?

After two years of a wide variety of project experiences among teachers, project manager volunteers, and students, an integrated set of methods and tools was consolidated into the *Project Management Kit for Primary School.*

In 2008, my story took another exciting turn, thanks to the PMI Congress in Malta, during which I had the opportunity to co-present the kit together with Mariù. It was a great challenge for both of us, but mainly for Mariù, who had to refresh her limited conversational English by undergoing a full immersion training in public speaking in English. Though it's hard to admit it, I know I could never have nearly the same level of courage and dedication as Mariù!

Among those in attendance at the presentation (my second lucky encounter) was Diane Fromm, a representative of the PMI Educational

Foundation who immediately shared our enthusiasm and started an intensive promotion of the *Kit for Primary School* through the PMI network.

Thanks to her, and to the direct and continuous support of the PMIEF board and staff, the following years were characterized by the gathering of a "dream team" of PMI chapter volunteers from four continents who provided the translation of the *Kit* in 13 different languages (with more translations to come!).

Thanks to them, more than half of the student population of our planet now has the possibility of learning and applying the project language and approach within the schools of their own countries—exciting proof of PMI's strategy of "thinking globally, acting locally."

And the lucky encounters along my exciting journey continued to occur.

The next one was with Giorgio Bensa, a Northern Italy Chapter volunteer who conceived and implemented an exciting annual school competition called *"Progetti in Erba"* ("Projects in Bloom"), that since 2010, has engaged students in dozens of schools in the northeastern region of Italy in applying project skills using our *Kit*.

In 2013, another passionate volunteer, Esther Cobos, promoted a humanitarian initiative funded by the PMIEF and aimed to provide free education and improved educational conditions for Congolese children.

Thanks to the Kubunina program (this word means "let's plan together" in the local Swahili language), 22 schools in the Congo and 22 sister schools in Italy had the opportunity to adopt the *Kit* as a common language to develop projects, exchange their results, and share lessons learned.

Also in 2013, I had another lucky encounter with Enrico Amiotti and his foundation dedicated to promoting and funding the professional development of primary school teachers. More than 50 Italian schools were provided with the opportunity to use the *Kit for Primary Schools* in an annual competition called *"Dal sogno al progetto"* ("From the dream to the project").

Last but not least, I have been honored by the participation of many hundreds of people—PMI volunteers, schoolteachers, and their students—who spent their best energies to experiment with and improve the *Kit*, and have gained the wonderful benefits of using project principles and practices in their teaching and learning. Thanks to them, project management has been promoted as both a life skill and a "universal language" for lifelong learning and productive work among new generations of 21st century learners and teachers.

What I have learned in my challenge of bridging project management and education is that lucky encounters may not be as "lucky" as I thought. When you are deeply involved in doing something important, inspirational leaders with similar dreams and visions are attracted to your project work and will often generously lend a helping hand in seeing your collective dream grow and prosper.

This is the great lesson from my deep friendship with Carlo and Georgio, because as Isaac Newton said:

> *If I have seen further than others, it is by standing upon the shoulders of a giants.*

This book is dedicated to Carlo and Giorgio who, though no longer with us, continue to inspire us all to bring to life their vision of project management skills for all students everywhere.

Project Manager Introduction

What Does Education Bring to Project Management?

*Between 2010 and 2020, 15.7 million new project management roles
will be created globally across seven project-intensive industries.*
—PMI Project Management Talent Gap Report (March 2013)

In 2013, a global survey of Project Management Institute's professionals
found that the market demand will create 15.7 million new project manager jobs in the decade 2010–2020, a growth rate of over 12%, accompa-
nied by a much fast than average growth rate in salaries.

So, will bringing project management to education in schools fill the
pipeline and close the gap between future demand and the supply of
new PM professionals?

One of the important missions of education is to prepare students
for careers and work demands of the future. But will integrating project management methods into our education systems create the needed
project-ready workforce of the future? The answer is not entirely straightforward, and the links between the education world and the business
world are complex and circular.

A simple lecture-based knowledge transfer to teachers and students from
project management business experts is clearly not enough to spread the
project language and methods to our young future workers. This would nei-
ther be effective instruction nor effective recruitment into the PM profession!

What is really needed is a "mutually influencing" relationship in
which both educators and project managers agree to be affected and
even changed by one another.

On one side, educators must have the courage to try out innovative
approaches to collaborative project learning, delegating more of the
project activities and leadership to their students, and acting as project
mentors and facilitators.

On the other side, PMs must adjust their language and perspective
to the education environment, not only by supporting the delivery of
the expected project deliverables, but by focusing their attention on

the effects that engaging school projects can have on students' learning motivation and the building of skills needed for life in the 21st century.

At the beginning of 2017, PMI announced a strategic change based upon a proposed aspirational mission statement for the times: "Improving the world through project leadership." As never in the past, this challenge is completely in sync with the PMIEF mission, which is to promote project management for social good.

To meet both of these challenging missions is not an unachievable dream. All project management practitioners can be champions who turn these words into realities for millions of students, educators, and for a brighter future for the project management profession and for project managers everywhere.

The Five Ps of Project Management for Education

> *I feel like every project I work on is a dream project,*
> *so long as I am learning.*
>
> **—Simeon Kondev**

There are many versions of lists of the key qualities of project management that often start with the letter P. Five of these "P-words" seem to best capture the essence of the mindsets and methods most central to adapting professional project management to the learning and teaching needs of students and educators, as illustrated here:

The 5Ps of Project Management for Education

The following is a brief outline of the most essential project practices in each of the 5P categories as an advance organizer and a "preview of coming attractions" that will be further explored in greater detail in the rest of the book:

- *People—manage the motivations, interactions, and teamwork*
  - Gain commitment of team members to the project goal
  - Manage the expectations of all project stakeholders
  - Communicate clearly and frequently with all project players
  - Collaborate productively and respectfully with all project members
  - Solve problems using effective critical and creative thinking

- *Process—apply proven project management strategies*
  - Follow best practices in each of the project cycle phases:
    - *Define* (Initiating)
    - *Plan* (Planning)
    - *Do* (Executing, Monitoring/Controlling)
    - *Review* (Closing)
  - Create a clear *Project Definition*
  - Commit to following the collaborative decisions in the *Teamwork Agreement*
  - Create, follow and update changes in the project *Work Plan*
  - Hold regular *Check-in Meetings* and record all updates and project changes
  - Evaluate and record progress during and at the close of a project for *Product* results, *Process* quality, and learning *Progress*

- *Products—create quality project work with strong impacts*
  - Keep overall quality of the craftsmanship of the project results as high as possible
  - Make sure project goals are achieved and the results are effective and useful
  - Seek feedback from the intended audience to ensure that expectations have been met

- ***Performance**—effectively manage the project process, product, and teamwork*
  - ○ Ensure the goals of the project are met
  - ○ Effectively manage all phases of the project cycle
  - ○ Meet all schedules and timelines
  - ○ Use all resources, tools, and materials productively and efficiently
  - ○ Effectively guide the implementation of all project updates and changes
  - ○ Respect the motivations and expectations of project members and stakeholders

And most important for applying project management methods to education, focus on:

- ***Progress** in Learning—deepen and broaden the learning gains for both students and educators*
  - ○ Track and celebrate gains in knowledge and expertise
  - ○ Recognize increases in skills and project performance
  - ○ Share reflections on growth in character qualities and motivation
  - ○ Honor competency gains in the ability to reflect, revise and plan further projects

There is an important difference between learning projects and most business projects, where the emphasis is often on being on time, on budget, and delivering exactly what is intended. In education, even if a project is not fully completed or takes longer than expected, and even if it uses more resources than expected, as long as the learning gains are truly significant for both individuals and project teams, the project may be considered a worthy and successful learning project. Always remember:

The learning gains from educational projects are the most important results!

Bringing Project Management to Schools, Educators, and Students

Why Is Project Management So Important to Student Success?

What's in It for Our Children?

> *The illiterate of the 21st century are not those who cannot read or write, but those who cannot learn, unlearn and relearn.*
> —**Alvin Toffler**

The question of "What's in it for our children?" is addressed not only to PMs who have children, but also to everyone who feels that helping all children be prepared for a successful future will make us all better off, now and well into the future.

That being said, to find a worthy answer to this question, it's appropriate to start with a quote from Richard Riley, sixth U.S. Secretary of Education, who said:

> *We are currently preparing students for jobs that don't yet exist, using technologies that haven't been invented, in order to solve problems we don't even know are problems yet.*

His message is clear and strong: Within an uncertain and rapidly changing world, the risk of one's current knowledge becoming quickly obsolete is very high. Young learners need to develop a wide selection of sharp "thinking and doing tools" for quickly analyzing complex problems, for conceiving and creating innovative solutions, and for effectively communicating and collaborating with other team members, all working together toward a clear goal. In other words, all students need to develop their competencies and supports to tackle complex questions, problems, or challenges through a project approach.

The good news is that school educators are becoming increasingly aware of this need for a dynamic and challenging learning approach in which students acquire deeper knowledge and skills through active exploration of real-world questions, problems, issues, and perspectives. The not-so-good news is that, in general, educators have very limited exposure or familiarity with the best practices of project management—practices that cannot be learned by reading a textbook or memorizing the key principles of the *Project Management Body of Knowledge* (the *PMBOK Guide*), but through direct experiences in managing and leading real learning projects with real students in real schools.

This "project experience gap" represents a tremendous opportunity for our community of project professionals to partner with schools, teachers, and educators everywhere to bring project learning experiences into the heart of education—collaborative project experiences that truly show the best of education and project management together.

With sturdy "*PM4Ed*" bridges in place, our future generations will be able to prevent the dangerous possibility that American futurist Alvin Toffler warned of in the quote at the top of this section. We can certainly add project learning literacy to the essential skills of the future.

Learning the principles and methods of effective project management holds the promise of bringing powerful sets of life skills, learning strategies, and career benefits to all students, enabling them to do more and better things in their lives, become lifelong self-motivated learners, and be highly productive and creative contributors in their school, family, work, career, and community lives.

What's in It for Project Managers?

Educating the mind without educating the heart is no education at all.
—**Aristotle**

Though accurate estimates are hard to come by, as of 2017 there are nearly a million certified project managers in the world. If you could count everyone who is regularly involved in managing projects in their work, with or without official certifications, that estimate could easily rise to well over 15 million PMs around the globe.

Projecting into the future, by 2025 the global number of PMs could reach more than 50 million, given the accelerating growth rate of the profession and the projected demand for project management capacity across all business sectors. One thing for sure, the demand for workers with project management expertise is clearly rising, and rising fast!

Though the compensation levels for project manager professionals is also high and rising, the job of being a project manager is not an easy or simple one. It involves daily challenges and multiple demands. PMs need to continuously and rapidly grow and deepen both their technical and people skills. Often, PMs are not fully recognized for the deep contributions they provide in creating successful organizational strategies and business successes.

Based on these observations, it is reasonable to ask whether PMs should invest time and energy to promote project based learning and project management in elementary and secondary schools. In addition to the good feelings generated by helping teachers and their students, what are the real benefits for the professional growth of those who have the everyday responsibilities of successfully managing "temporary endeavors undertaken to create a unique product, service, or result"—the essence of projects?

The answer to this question can be found in the above-mentioned challenge that many PMs face in receiving the full recognition for their contributions to business and strategy success. To stay motivated, PMs must achieve a goal that is personally as important as meeting their project goals: to be recognized, not only as experts in a body of knowledge, but also as open-minded and caring professionals who have the ability to adapt their project language and methods into the common language and culture of the organizations in which they work.

The project language is flexible and intuitive for thinking about and accomplishing things—a language that can be spoken by all stakeholders regardless of their position in their organizations' hierarchies, a language that enables everyone to benefit from the best talents and skills available, a language that is the foundation of collective leadership and collaborative teamwork.

Now, if this goal of teaching and reaching as many as possible with the benefits of the project language and project principles and practices is really important for a PM, the possibility of bringing these gifts to students and educators represents an extraordinary opportunity to become more:

- Aware of how the project language is agile and easily adaptable to all levels of education;
- Impressed that young learners, even in the first grades of primary school, are able to develop creative and critical thinking through the use of simple project methods and tools, such as brainstorming and mind mapping;
- Admired by educators and students for providing such simple and powerful organizing tools such as the *Work Breakdown Structure*, from which even young students using simple versions can benefit;
- Surprised by the unself-conscious excitement children express when they are able to organize their activities on the basis of team agreements and ground rules of their own design; and
- Deeply moved by students' new awareness and surprises, such as a nine-year-old student who suddenly realized, "Even the shiest children felt involved and took part in our project's teamwork."

From so many reports of PM's positive volunteering experiences supporting project based learning in schools, colleges, and universities, it is clear that PMs can bring positive learning and beneficial changes to students, teachers, and schools, and, in turn, become more aware of the power of projects for student learning, more influential in their ability to spread the power of project practices, more able to embrace complexity (such as the culture of school classrooms), and much more. Simply put, bringing one's expertise to the world of education makes a PM a *more dedicated professional*.

There are many ways to bring the benefits of these education experiences back into one's everyday work world, and in particular, within project management training. Examples of successful school projects can be used as "ice breakers" in a basic project management training course, or as an effective way to compare the principles of "agile" project approaches (e.g., iterative planning, self-organizing teams, etc.) with the methods of project based learning used in schools.

Another response to the "What's in it for me?" question can be related to both the strong need for self-motivation in PM work and the desire to constantly improve leadership and communication skills.

A PM, by definition, is the main hub of each project network. As a result, a PM's motivation level can deeply influence team members and other stakeholders, including the project sponsor.

The experience of educational volunteering has a profound influence on the deep motivating agents—the "intrinsic motivators"—that propel our project work and our careers forward.

Daniel Pink, author of *Drive: The Surprising Truth About What Motivates Us*, overturns the conventional wisdom about human motivation that the best way to motivate people is with external rewards such as money and "carrot-and-stick" methods. His research reveals that three "intrinsic motivators" offer a much more effective path: autonomy, mastery, and purpose.

The way to better performance and satisfaction—at work, at school, and at home—rests on the deeply human need to direct our own lives, to learn and create new things, and to serve others and a cause much larger than ourselves.

Now, if these motivating factors are really decisive for the professional growth and success of a PM, school volunteering may be the best "exercise gym" to practice and develop these "motivational muscles" because:

- *Autonomy* is assured—a PM is free to choose when and how the collaboration with educators and school directors will occur;
- *Mastery* is assured—a PM is strongly stimulated to think out of the box within a vital and dynamic environment such as a local school or community program and bring her/his expertise and mastery of project management to new levels of understanding; and
- *Purpose* is assured—a PM is fully rewarded by the satisfaction of making a direct contribution to the local community and

helping to make learning more engaging, meaningful, and useful throughout a young person's life.

This is exactly what is happening to passionate and motivated PMs all over the world. Thanks to many of you, and many more to come, this double benefit—one, for improving the learning lives of students, and two, for increasing the motivation and professionalism of a PM—will become a regular part of the professional and leadership development of all PMs.

Project Management as Learning, Work, and Life Skills

How Can Learning Projects Help All Students Become More Successful?

Thinking about the PMs and professionals who are reading this book (let's hope there are many!), the most appropriate answer to "How can we help all students become more successful?" may best come from those PMs who have actually worked with students and teachers over long periods of time, maturing their outlook on what is most effective in supporting teachers and students in their learning projects.

How have these successful PMs made a difference in bringing project management to education?

The simple answer is the one suggested by American futurist Alvin Toffler as how to best cope with an unknown future—by "learning, un-learning and re-learning."

The example most familiar to this project manager author (Walter) is my own experience of over 10 years working in schools. The following is my personal story, but one that will undoubtedly be similar but still unique to other PMs who are bridging the worlds of project management and education.

My goal is not to provide a detailed picture of a structured approach to project based learning (PBL) for schools; rather, my goal is to show the path that allowed me to understand the deeper meaning of PBL ("why"), to design a project cycle compliant with the learning processes of the students ("how"), and, finally, to select the best set of tools and techniques needed to deliver the expected product or result ("what").

Why?—Projects as a Model for Building Life Skills

As of 2007, after the pilot projects I developed in three primary schools in my city of Milan, I started a promotional campaign to spread the word about these first successful experiences and to respond to the interest many school teachers and directors who heard of these early successes expressed.

I must confess that their reactions at the end of my presentations were not always completely positive and encouraging.

In some cases, they showed a sort of diffidence about my proposal of a new PBL experiment; in others, they expressed interest coupled with a large amount of skepticism.

I tried to justify their reactions as the typical resistance to change of those facing something unfamiliar, who already had a great deal of existing work on their plate, and a clear desire not to increase any uncertainty in their status or role as a teacher or principal.

But, looking back over my 10-year journey, this was clearly not the most common reason for their reactions. There were two reasons why my thinking was incorrect:

- *First of all, the wide majority of school teachers, and primary school teachers in particular, is open to contribute to pilot projects of new learning approaches, especially those that really engage the hearts and minds of students.*
- *Second, a large number of motivated and experienced teachers is fully aware that her/his mission is not only to perform a knowledge transfer of information, but also to enable each student to become a self-directed learner who can acquire the ability of "learning to learn." In other words, they know that teaching is a creative profession aimed at getting students to become independent learners, and not a delivery system based upon efficient information transmission and standardized testing of memory.*

In short, today I can say that the main cause of those early misunderstandings and communication blockers at the beginning of my collaboration with the school world was not a result of the educators' re-sistance to change, but rather was because of my limited comprehension of their true answer to the question of "why" to even consider applying project management best practices in a classroom of K–12 students.

In fact, if I go back to my first presentations, I remember that I used to focus on the need to prepare students for their future jobs, especially with the increasing demand for project management practitioners by private and public organizations.

This implied that, in order to engage school representatives, I was dealing with the "why" issue, not from the perspective of an educator, but only from my perspective of a project manager who thinks project management is a sort of "proprietary language" for the business world.

How could I have altered this too simplistic vision of project management for education, and on whose benefit should I have been really focusing? The benefit must be recognized by the team of school teachers, including my wife, Mariù, with whom I have been so lucky to collaborate on the design and validation of the school toolkit.

Thanks to their help, I have become fully aware of two facts that are strongly interrelated:

- *First, students' learning and life skills are extremely important to all teachers, whose day-to-day efforts are aimed at ensuring a progressive and harmonic improvement of these skills, both at the individual and collective levels.*
- *Second, adopting learning projects doesn't mean adding a new discipline (project management) into the school curriculum, but instead using simple project language (that's not business proprietary) as an effective tool for stimulating and improving students' learning strategies and everyday life skills.*

In addition, I discovered that learning, work, and life skills, or 21st century skills as they are often called, are the focus of educational interest in many governmental institutions, both global and local.

In my research on these skills, I found three reference models that are particularly meaningful:

- *The first one, conceived in 1993 by the World Health Organization (WHO), defined life skills as "abilities for adaptive and positive behaviors that enable individuals to effectively deal* with demands and challenges of everyday life." Within this framework, the WHO identified a set of 10 abilities (listed in the chart below).

- The second one, issued in 2006 as part of the Strategy of Lisbon (an initiative to modernize education in Europe), contained a set of recommendations aimed at ensuring that Europe's citizens can acquire a wide range of key competences to face a rapidly changing and highly interconnected world. This European framework identifies eight key competences for lifelong learning (listed below).

- The third one, designed by the United States–based Partnership for 21st Century Skills (or P21—now the Partnership for 21st Century Learning), selected a set of four key competences to be adopted and implemented into the curricula of schools, school districts, and professional development programs. This framework is the Four Cs of 21ˢᵗ Century Learning, or "The Four Cs" for short.

The following table summarizes the key competencies identified within each reference model.

Life Skills Competencies Reference Models

Source: United Nations (WHO)	Source: European Parliament	Source: P21 (U.S.-based)
1. Decision making	1. Communication in the mother tongue	1. Creative thinking
2. Problem solving	2. Communication in foreign languages	2. Critical thinking
3. Creative thinking	3. Competence in math, science, and technology	3. Communication
4. Critical thinking	4. Digital competence	4. Collaboration
5. Effective communication	5. Learning to learn	
6. Interpersonal relationship skills	6. Social and civic competences	
7. Self-awareness	7. Sense of initiative and entrepreneurship	
8. Empathy	8. Cultural awareness and expression	
9. Coping with emotions		
10. Coping with stress		

While keeping in mind differences and similarities among these edu-cational reference frameworks, I must admit that the Four Cs model has been a real breakthrough for me, because it has allowed me to understand the deep meaning of learning through projects and to change my engage-ment strategy toward school stakeholders.

As a matter of fact, if it's true that creative and critical thinking, communication, and collaboration are essential for the future, it's also true that the experience of a project developed in a classroom is a sort of "workout gym" where these four key competencies can emerge and be strengthened. Projects and the 4Cs are intimately related simply because:

- *A project is aimed at delivering something new and unique, an objective that calls for creativity, intuition, and the ability to think outside of the box, both individually and collectively;*
- *A project calls for the search of working solutions, compatible with time and resource constraints, a need that demands crit-ical thinking and problem solving;*
- *Being a human adventure, project success relies upon effective communications among the involved stakeholders, for which it's necessary to adopt appropriate styles and common tools in order to avoid the Tower of Babel syndrome of misunderstood messages; and*
- *Being a human adventure, project success also relies on effec-tive teamwork and, therefore, strong and empathetic collabo-ration skills motivated by a set of common project goals.*

Understanding this clearer educational perspective of the "why" of project management as a lifelong and life-wide skill, I can now provide some helpful advice to those volunteers (I hope there are many) who are interested in spreading project principles and practices in the schools of their countries:

1. *During kick-off meetings with school teachers, try to avoid initial questions and discussions solely based upon a project manager's perspective, such as: "What do you think about project management and its application in the classroom?"*

2. *On the contrary, try to base introductory questions on the teacher's perspective, such as: "On the basis of your experience, do you think that a project is a good learning practice that can stimulate and strengthen your students' life skills?"*

Believe me, school teachers will unanimously reply: "Yes, we do," and their positive answer is one of the foundations of building bridges between project management and education.

How?—A Project Cycle for Learning Projects

After the first pilot projects developed in 2006, my long collaboration with primary school teachers continued in 2007 with a kick-off meeting aimed at laying the foundations of a project framework suitable for children from 6 to 11 years of age. Thanks to the fact that my wife was part of that team, two things were very clear in my mind:

- *First, I was aware that the use of projects as a learning opportunity for students was already being practiced in many ways and in various subjects, from the development of a scientific or historical research project, to the creation of a "lab" for artistic or theatrical performances; from the setup of an exhibition of artifacts made by the children, to organizing the celebration of important events such as a party at the end of the school year.*
- *Second, I was equally aware that each teacher was following her/his own approach to launch a school project, to assign roles and responsibilities to the students, to monitor the execution, and provide the needed adjustments in case of changes for unexpected events. In other words, it was as if the teacher had in mind a project charter, a WBS, and a sort of plan whose activities were assigned to the responsibility of a student or group of students.*

Against this background, I was confronted by a small dilemma: Should I design a project cycle by starting from an existing well-researched reference such as the PMBOK, or should I codesign something new with the schoolteachers by starting from a blank sheet of paper, but informed by the basic components of the standard project cycle?

Thanks to the lessons learned in the pilot phase, I was convinced that the second option was best because of my conviction that teachers must be a part of discovering the "why" and must participate in the defining phases of a project so that they would "buy in" and commit to the project approach.

I decided to rely on the real-life experience of the teachers involved by asking them to conceive of an effective way to explain the idea of a project to a classroom of children by showing them the phases needed to pass from an idea to its implementation.

Today, I can say that it was a very good choice. After the decision to adopt the metaphor of a journey as an appropriate description of a project, the teachers started the design of a very intuitive project cycle based on the following four phases:

- *Creation—the children set their imagination free and express ideas and wishes about an adventure trip. Gradually, the teacher supports them while they make choices related to their destinations, fellow travelers, ground rules, etc.*
- *Planning—now the trip needs to be organized. Nothing must be overlooked and specific responsibilities and duties must be assigned to each member of the team for everything to be ready, including the route to follow for the sailing date.*
- *Execution and Control—the trip has begun. Every day may bring some surprises; the route can be adjusted, but the destination remains the same. The compass helps keep the direction.*
- *Closing—the trip has come to an end and the destination has been reached. Now the logbook is reviewed and, with the help of the teacher, a story of the lessons learned is constructed out of it, which is sure to be of use in other trips.*

These four parts of the project are captured in these project cycle visualizations:

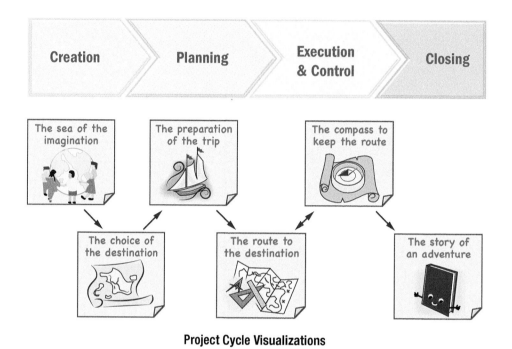

Project Cycle Visualizations

Thanks to this intuition, a methodological framework for the primary school began to take shape and then, through many revisions and extensions, it became the visual Project Management Toolkit *that currently is available in 14 languages.*

But what is really astounding about this teachers' teamwork is the discovery I made a few years later when I had the opportunity at a conference to first meet my now friend and collaborator on this book, Bernie Trilling, and was introduced to the project model he helped develop for PMIEF in collaboration with the Partnership for 21st Century Skills. *The model has a sequence of four phases (Define, Plan, Do, Review) very similar to those conceived by a group of educators on the other side of the ocean. This apparent coincidence dissolved all my doubts about the universality of the project language that is most appropriate for schools.*

Is this only a coincidence? I don't think so. It's simply further evidence that the project language is a universal language and that school teachers all over the world are becoming more and more aware of its potential as a life skill. In my opinion, this increasing awareness can represent the central pillar of the bridge between project management and education.

What?—Seven Visual Tools for Thinking and Doing

Having faced and resolved the questions related to the "why" and "how", the team of teachers I was working with was then assisted by some volunteers from the PMI Northern Italy Chapter *in an attempt to identify, experiment, and validate a set of intuitive techniques and tools to be used within the four-phase project cycle.*

Because of their deep experience with all kinds of students, we asked the teacher to come up with a list of essential requirements in order to ensure the consistency and effectiveness of the whole Project Management Toolkit for Primary Schools.

Starting from the four-part project cycle, the first suggestion the teachers had was to promote the use of "visual" tools as an effective means to ensure the highest flexibility and "agility" in helping students quickly understand the processes, and above all, to facilitate the sharing of the ideas.

As a second requirement, teachers expressed their preference for two techniques that were very familiar to them: Brainstorming—*as a powerful way to enable creativity and divergent thinking, and* Mind Mapping—*as an intuitive way to enable convergent thinking and integrating the ideas generated through* Brainstorming.

With regard to Mind Mapping, *the teachers suggested using a template containing predefined branches that corresponded to the key questions of a project, such as "Why?" (objectives), "Who?" (stakeholders), "When?" (target date), "Where?" (location), and so on. In addition, they included two very important branches:*

- *A "What?" branch, as a container for project deliverables that are essential to deriving the project activities through the typical top-down process of decomposition; and*
- *A "What if?" branch, as a brilliant solution to stimulate students to think about risks and opportunities (providing further room for their creativity and imagination).*

As far as the planning phase is concerned, the teachers welcomed the proposal of the local PMI *chapter's experts concerning the use of two typical tools of a project manager: the* Work Breakdown Structure (WBS) *and the* Network Diagram *(an adaptation of the Gantt Chart that uses Post-it sticky notes).*

Once again, the teachers provided a meaningful contribution in terms of a simplified language by stressing the need to avoid overly technical terms that are not suitable for primary school children. For this reason, they suggested to translate the term Work Breakdown Structure *into* "Project Tree", *a choice that was immediately adopted, because a WBS is really nothing more than a tree diagram.*

For the Network Diagram *that is built with the "leaves" of the* Project Tree *(the so-called work packages), the teachers' choice was to adopt the term* Project Calendar, *a structured list in which students can put activities ("What to do") in serial or parallel sequences ("When?").*

As an example of how constraints often motivate the search for creative solutions, the teachers had a new brilliant idea for the execution phase.

In fact, they proposed the use of "project traffic lights" as visual representations of the completion of each deliverable (interestingly, no teacher had a clue about the project management dashboards that are typically used in the business context and serve the same visual messaging needs for professionals!).

With regard to the closing phase, the educators pointed out its paramount importance, not only as an essential moment of celebration of the entire project experience, but also as a great opportunity for students to reflect on their learning progress (also interestingly, no teacher had a clue about the typical lack of attention to the closing phase in the business context!).

Bearing in mind the process and its objectives, it was suggested to use a Mind Map *with a set of branches corresponding to questions such as: "What did I learn?", "What could I do better?", "What was the most difficult thing?", and so forth.*

In this way, each student and the whole classroom are stimulated to reflect upon the project experiences with the collected feedback displayed on sticky notes for all to see. This is undoubtedly the most important project deliverable for both the teacher and students.

Last but not least, when the joint effort to explore the "what" seemed to be over, the PMs of the team highlighted the absence of a key document—the Project Charter *containing objectives, time and cost constraints, involved stakeholders, expected results, etc.*

As a confirmation of the strength of the peer-to-peer relationships among the educator project practitioners, the teachers recognized the need for this document by suggesting to name it the "Project Identity Card" and, in addition, to integrate it with a set of "Ground Rules" that students must share and respect from the project kick-off to the close, such as practicing active listening, supporting one another when difficulties arise, and so on.

As a confirmation of the universality of the project language, I invite PMs to look for interesting articles about the "Team Charter", a specific document in which team members can describe their raison d'être, their goals or mission as a group, their roles as individuals within the team, and the operating agreement under which the entire team will work.

I strongly hope that these "curious coincidences" will be enough to demonstrate that the bridge between project management and education isn't a utopian fiction but a solid reality that can be constructively built together.

This is the "why", "how", and "what" journey that I traveled into the world of education—an extraordinary trip with a team of passionate volunteers and motivated schoolteachers that led to the conception, design, and validation of an integrated set of seven visual tools for thinking and doing. Those tools are represented in the following illustration:

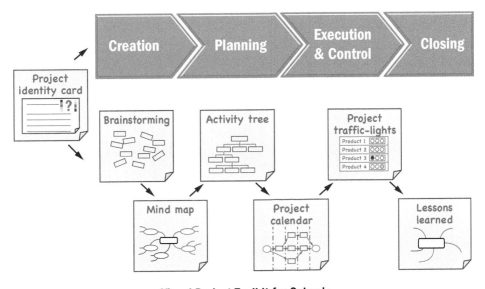

Visual Project Toolkit for Schools

Proposed Project Management Toolkit Extensions

Thanks to the generous effort of many PMI volunteers, not only in Italy, but also in other countries (Portugal, Slovenia, France, Turkey, Mexico, Taiwan, Kuwait, Congo, etc.), the Project Management Toolkit for Primary School *has been successfully experimented with in more than 100 K–12 schools.*

With regard to the secondary schools, PMI volunteers have provided a set of adjustments and extensions to the basic Toolkit version in terms of activities, documents, tools, and techniques. In this way, secondary school students are helped to address more complex issues, such as stakeholder analysis, time and cost estimation, risk assessment and response planning, schedule optimization, and so on.

Even if these experiences have not been integrated yet in a unique framework, as it has occurred for the primary school, I'd like to exploit the opportunity of this book to send a message to the project management community and to PMI volunteers throughout the world:

> Why don't we share an inter-chapter program aimed at building the extension of the school toolkit through the same approach followed for the Government-Software-Construction Extension to the *PMBOK*?

The following table is a first proposal with the only goal of engaging many open-minded volunteers who are available to accept this challenge:

Proposed Project Management Toolkit Extensions

Phase	Step	Basic Toolkit for Primary School	Activities & Tools Extension for Middle/Secondary School
Creation (DEFINE)	1.	Project identity card	☞ Conduct a stakeholder analysis and define the best engagement strategy ♦ Stakeholder register and, if needed, stakeholder grid (power and interest)
	2.	Brainstorming	☞ Interact with the involved stakeholders and collect their needs and requirements ♦ Interviews, questionnaires, surveys
	3.	Mind map	☞ Explore the economical dimension through a new branch: "how much?" (project costs) ♦ Estimate project budget and, if needed, costs breakdown (fixed, variable, etc.)
Planning (PLAN)	4.	Activity tree	☞ Identify project risks and the appropriate response strategy (avoid, mitigate, etc.) ♦ Risk register and probability and impact matrix
	5.	Project calendar	☞ Calculate the project duration and, if needed, optimize the project plan ♦ Critical path method, Gantt chart
Execution & Control (DO)	6.	Project traffic-lights Product 1 Product 2 Product 3 Product 4	☞ Evaluate the project performance with regard to planned durations and costs ♦ Estimate time and cost at completion
Closing (REVIEW)	7.	Lessons learned	☞ Discuss and evaluate problems encountered during the project ♦ Root-cause analysis

During 10 years of volunteering within primary schools, I have interviewed many teachers in order to collect evaluations about their PBL experience and its effects on students' 4Cs life skills. In the following Skills Developed in the Project Cycle table, I've summarized their feedback as a concluding answer to the initial question of this chapter: "How can learning projects help all students become more successful?"

Student Skills Developed in the Project Cycle

Phase	Creative Thinking	Critical Thinking	Communication	Collaboration	Schoolteachers' evaluations about how students' life skills are positively impacted by a project experience
Creation (DEFINE)	☑				Ideation and design of the project logo and choice of an engaging name for the project identity card
		☑			Evaluation and selection of the ideas generated during the brainstorming on the basis of their feasibility
			☑		Active listening to other students' ideas and careful use of an appropriate language to express their own ideas
				☑	Being able to integrate one's ideas with other ideas and also to encourage others to express their ideas
Planning (PLAN)	☑				Effort of imagination aimed at identifying alternative ways to generate the same products or results
		☑			Use of deductive reasoning in order to derive project activities starting from expected outputs (deliverables)
			☑		Ability to ask or provide explanations and clarifications in order to describe project activities in the best way
				☑	Discuss and negotiate possible solutions and be open to accept and share responsibilities and roles
Execution & Control (DO)	☑				Search of alternative solutions in cases where students are faced with large delays or unexpected events
		☑			Evaluation of the project status and identification of the needed adjustments of the project tree and calendar
			☑		Ability to describe situations with objectivity and to ask for assistance in front of difficulty or contingency
				☑	Being available to work with different teams and ready to support other teams in case of problems or delays
Closing (REVIEW)	☑				Reflections upon new projects on the basis of results and lessons learned thanks to the completed project
		☑			Trying to imagine the results that would be obtained if the project team had taken different decisions
			☑		Ability to recount personal and collective experiences and report them clearly (who, when, why, what, etc.)
				☑	Use the experience to reinforce the sense of belonging to the team in anticipation of future similar projects

School Projects Versus Business Projects

What Do They Have in Common? What's Different?

What They Have in Common

At the end of one of many project based learning experiences, an expert project based high school teacher put this question to her students:

> *After all of your experiences in doing learning projects, would you mind telling me what a project really is?*

To add some structure to the students' feedback, she asked them to collectively identify the 10 most important attributes of a project, including a short description for each of the key attributes.

The following are the students' surprising collective responses to this challenge.

They said that projects are:

1. *Temporary:* "They have a beginning and an end;"
2. *Innovative:* "They generate something new;"
3. *Finalized:* "They're aimed at achieving a goal;"
4. *Concrete:* "They deliver useful results;"
5. *Progressive:* "They become more and more clear along the way;"

6. *Collaborative:* "They imply more teamwork and less hierarchy;"
7. *Risky:* "They always involve uncertainty;"
8. *Transparent:* "They demand continuous open communication;"
9. *Reusable:* "They are a source of useful new knowledge;" and
10. *Unique:* "Only we did it!"

Why is this student-generated list of project attributes so surprising?

- First, because the list contains both of the key concepts included in the official PMI *Project Management Body of Knowledge (PMBOK)* definition of a project—the *temporary* nature of a project (first attribute) and the fact that the product, service, or result delivered by a project is always *unique* (last attribute);
- Second, because all listed attributes are fully compliant with a typical business project, even though they came from the learning and life experiences of 16-year-old high school students;
- Third, because the students understood the importance of two attributes that many international surveys put at the top of the critical success factors of a project: *collaboration* (sixth attribute) and *communication* (eighth attribute); and
- Last but not least, because the students understood the strong connection between project management and knowledge management (ninth attribute); this is probably the most surprising attribute, because there is no way they could have known that among the updates planned for the upcoming sixth edition of the *PMBOK*, there is the addition of a new integration process called "Manage Project Knowledge."

So, are there really no significant differences between school projects and business projects?

A further analysis based on the diverse experiences of a wide variety of teachers in different schools and grade levels may help answer this question.

How They Are Different

The following represents a summary of interviews involving a wide population of teachers in an attempt to identify the elements of project management that are particular to school projects. This doesn't mean that they are not applicable to the context of business projects. On the contrary, many of these differentiators must be considered food for deeper thought by PMs who want to explore the wider and deeper meanings of the concept of "project" and the evolving practices of the project management profession.

There are four elements that a wide majority of teachers indicate are key success factors in the processes important to learning projects— learning is a journey, look beyond the deliverables, the emerging project charter, and projects as an emotional investment—all explained below.

Learning Is a Journey, Not a Destination

Thanks to the PMIEF, which provided funds for a humanitarian project in Africa, 22 Italian schools and 22 Congolese schools had the opportunity to collaborate and share the results of their projects. Students in a primary school in Milan designed and built a puppet theater that was sent to their friends in their Congolese sister school.

During one of the learning sessions, one of the Italian students remarked, "Luca's grandfather made the puppet theater's textile walls, Elia's grandmother sewed the puppet clothes, Mariù's husband provided the puppet theater's aluminium structure. But in the end, what did we students do?"

Immediately, other students spoke up: "We were the ones that did the project and, without us, the theater wouldn't have been delivered to our friends in the Congo."

The important lesson learned, from the perspective of an educator, is that the project results are not as important as the journey of getting there. In practice, each single phase or task of a school project represents a fundamental step in the learning process, a way to practice building interpersonal relationships, an opportunity to build essential life skills, and a chance to widen perceptions of the world.

Even parents noticed this effect. A father, after seeing his young son's work, asked the teacher how he could transfer the project management skills the students learned to his own workers at a research institute.

What do these stories show us, as project managers?

We are rarely fully aware that at the end of a highly engaging collaborative learning project with deep meaning and strong impacts for all involved, all participants, especially the supportive volunteer project manager, will not be the same by the end of the project. Very probably, the contributing PMs will become better caring persons and stronger motivated professionals.

> *So, let's learn from teachers and students about how projects can be learning journeys of transformative personal growth and development.*

Always Look Beyond the Deliverables

Egle, a primary school teacher, is one of the "veterans" who have been practicing project based learning since 2010.

A few years ago, she offered this story with the typical pride of a passionate educator:

> *On the occasion of my birthday, my pupils gave me a nice handicraft made by them. It was a surprise, but the true surprise was to discover that they had planned everything through a set of sticky notes put on a calendar.*

Another similar story comes from the mother of Carlo, a 10-year-old student. It started with a school problem that Carlo's older brother had, concerning a geography research project he was to complete with a group of reluctant classmates.

Carlo's suggestion to his brother was immediate and confident:

> *Don't worry; just start with some brainstorming and then create a mind map with all your ideas.*

His suggestion was to keep calm and use the project language and methods he learned at school.

These two short anecdotes show that what really matters for educators is not only for their pupils to internalize the project approach, but that they also are able to apply it spontaneously to other situations, even outside the classroom. Managing a much broader portfolio of projects than many PMs, educators are much more focused on the post-project personal benefits to their students rather than project deliverables.

This doesn't mean that the quality of project results is not important in school projects compared to business projects. It simply means that learning projects have a high demand for change management, including the need for an "extended" view of the project cycle and longer-term impacts.

What is the important message educators are sending to PMs?

The more we are able to look beyond the delivery of project results to wider impacts, the more successful our professional projects will be, and the more motivated and engaged our teams, our sponsors, and all the project stakeholders will be.

The "Emerging Project Charter"

During a training course on the *Project Management ToolKit for Primary School*, an explanation was being presented on the first step in the project life cycle—sharing a *"Project Identity Card,"* a sort of simplified project charter containing basic elements such as name, logo, goals, expected results, and ground rules for the team.

At the end of the explanation, one of the teachers highlighted the need for a more flexible approach to allow integrating and completing all the *Project Identity Card* elements during the next project steps (*Brainstorming, Mind Mapping*, etc.). She was making the case for a "progressive elaboration" of the project definition.

The reason for this request, she said, was that the abstraction process of a child is very different from that of an adult. Younger students need living concrete experiences to then move gradually to an understanding of and an ability to speak about higher-level concepts, such as project goals or ground rules. In addition, as these concrete experiences are acquired, children start to engage their emotions and their creative juices to come up with innovative project names, inspiring logos, and so on.

The mentoring project manager at first considered this a peculiarity of school projects that was not applicable to business projects. Shortly thereafter, the project manager mentor saw a research report on project complexity aimed at bringing together academic, military, and business worlds to explore project management in highly complex, volatile, and uncertain situations using, appropriately enough, "complexity theory."

Among the research findings published in these reports, the idea of an "emerging project charter" was offered as a tool for mitigating the typical uncertainty and unpredictability in very complex projects. In other words, this tool was aimed at tracking all the evolutions of the project while its phases unfolded and emerging deliverables were identified, designed, and created.

The teacher who suggested the progressive elaboration of the *Project Identity Card* was clearly not a member of the research team, but her astute observations demonstrated that the apparent differences between school and business projects may dissolve when one looks deeper into the realities of managing projects in diverse and dynamic environments such as school classrooms!

Projects as Emotional Investments

During post-project evaluation meetings to review projects results and benefits, many teachers from different grades have emphasized the need to take into account the emotional effects of school projects on their students. In particular, primary school teachers have strongly asserted the need for children to have clear, positive, and encouraging responses from their teachers and classmates to stay engaged and motivated.

All students must be actively involved—in thinking, feeling, and doing—in all project phases, be recognized for their roles and contributions, be actively listened to, be aware of the responsibilities they have in carrying out their own tasks, and, last but not least, be appreciated for their particular contributions to their project successes.

Almost all actions of teachers and mentors must include a critical goal: to maximize the "ROEI" (Return on Emotional Investment) for each individual student and the whole project team as well.

Taking all of the points of "difference" above, one must ask professional PMs: "Are these real differences?" Don't excellent PMs, as true servant leaders, practice similar project methods to those that these educators practice, or at least, feel that they should do so? Do some business projects fail to generate economical ROI because they have ignored the ROEI?

One conclusion that can be offered based on this review is that school projects can be the best metaphors for exemplary business projects.

There is much to learn about the finer points of project management from educators and students!

Project Management and Time Management

How Can We Help Others Tackle This Lifelong Motivational Challenge?

Every millisecond someone downloads an app from Apple's App Store. Every couple of minutes Apple sells another of its devices to a customer. The orders whip through Apple's inventory system and are delivered in four days. Apple's product updates and new product launches happen around every four weeks or less.

A few time measures from a popular tech company are not nearly enough to fully grasp how much the pace of change is accelerating in our world and, as a consequence, how time management has become a lifelong challenge for our "always-on" connected lives.

Looking at this challenge from the perspective of an educator or school administrator, one wonders what responsibility schools and teachers have to help their students manage the rush of an accelerating world where answers to questions are instantly available and the choices about how to use one's time seem almost infinite (while being constantly interrupted by tweets and text messages in social media).

Managing time is also a great challenge for teachers. This challenge raises lots of important questions:

- How should teachers divide their time between the needs of individual students versus the demands of a whole classroom?

27

- How much time should teachers spend learning from other teachers (if collaboration time is available) or from professional development in workshops and classes versus working on their own lessons and project plans for their students?
- How should teachers divide their time between family responsibilities at home and reviewing and grading student work after school?
- How much time should teachers spend on reports required by the school and district (with often nonnegotiable deadlines)?

And on top of all these time challenges that a "school project manager" faces each day, the expectations of students' parents are constantly growing, along with new demands for providing more advanced curricula, including emerging topics such as environmental sustainability, relationships with other cultures, ethical issues, and so on.

It's clear that a schoolteacher is just as impacted by time challenges and constraints as a project management practitioner in the business world, if not even more so.

With few options to expand the school calendar time, the workload of teachers continues to increase, along with the demands of students, parents, and administrators, while the number of hours in the day (including sleep time) remain permanently fixed.

Amazingly, the passion, commitment, and professionalism of so many dedicated educators are what keeps teachers doing what they can to help all of their students gain the skills they need for future success, and the only factor that prevents teachers from rushing to get through their lessons and the school day or, even worse, constantly interrupting their work with students at a critical moment in the students' learning process.

But what about the challenges teachers' students are facing each day? What can teachers do to help their students manage their own time pressures and stress, which seem to be on a perilous rise in so many places? How can teachers (and students' parents) help students cope with the increasing 21st century demands on their time?

Though teachers are committed to raising students' awareness about the impacts of time management on their lives (just as they are keenly aware of the impacts on their own lives) they also know that changing students' perceptions and behaviors around the use of time is not easy.

Teachers understand that the common "student syndrome"—students' natural tendency to procrastinate schoolwork until the last possible moment before its deadline—is almost impossible to change (teachers often suffer from the same syndrome in their own work). They also know the stress this creates in students when all time safety margins are progressively eliminated until the point of no return is passed and there is not enough time left to complete the tasks.

The tendency to procrastinate is not just a school syndrome. In the business world, the "critical chain" method, whose goal is to protect project schedules through the identification and insertion of project, feeding, and resource "buffers," fully recognizes the widespread inclination for procrastination and takes this into account.

How can educators help students overcome this natural and universal tendency to put things off to the last minute, and how can project based learning (PBL) positively affect the time management ability of students by helping them tackle this lifelong motivational challenge?

Kenneth Lovell, an English Methodist and pioneer in mathematics education, tackled the question of time management in a book entitled *The Growth of Basic Mathematical and Scientific Concepts in Children*. Some of his thoughts on the subject included the following ideas:

- We cannot be sure about how to teach children the concept of time.
- Nonetheless it's quite probable that observing and focusing on activities with clear beginnings and ends can generate learning opportunities to better understand the phenomenon of time.
- When the concept of time is well developed, we can invite students to estimate time intervals of a variety of processes, providing opportunities to become better time estimators.

Taking inspiration from Lovell's statements and from the reflections of many teachers who grapple with how to impart an understanding of managing time to their students, it seems clear that experiencing a learning project in a classroom can offer a sort of "gym workout" in which students can practice and become better at time management.

Each element of a project can generate positive understandings and behaviors related to time, with the indispensable support of passionate and open-minded teachers. These elements include the following:

- Each project is characterized by a start and end date. This means that at the same time a teacher is facilitating a project kick-off, students can be stimulated to think about time constraints and objectives to be achieved within a shared time period.
- Each project implies the identification of activities to be done (what), the people assigned to them (who), and the days/weeks/months estimated for the delivery (when). In this context, students are pushed to imagine how those activities can be executed and, as a consequence, evaluate the time needed for their completion.
- Each project requires that activities be scheduled by taking into account preceding activities and activity sequences. These constraints can represent a further stimulation for the students because they can easily realize that a potential delay for an activity assigned to someone else (or to another team) can generate negative propagation effects to the activities assigned to others.
- Each project is characterized by periodic reviews of the work done and, if needed, small or big adjustments in the original plan. From the perspective of the students' learning processes, the effects of these reviews can be extremely positive. First of all, they represent an opportunity for students to verify the initial estimates and reflect upon variances, their work, and their motivations. Second, each adjustment to the current plan always implies an evaluation of the time factor and the possibility of completing the project within the target date.
- Each project should be closed with an ex-post analysis of the experience gained, knowledge acquired, and lessons learned to be capitalized in future projects. For a teacher, this is undoubtedly the most important step of a project based learning initiative. Therefore, it represents a precious opportunity to engage all students in a collective reflection upon time management and its effects.

In Greek mythology, two gods represented two different ways of living the experience of time:

- *Chrónos* represented chronological time—that is, serial time, measurable by external clocks and chronometers, and corresponding to a sequence of dots over a line; and
- *Kairós* represented cyclical or experiential time, not measurable by clocks, and related to the internal perceptions of human intentions, propositions, and circumstances.

The ability to manage both types of time is a distinctive skill, not only for a project management practitioner, but also for a passionate educator who knows perfectly well that Chrónos has to do with planning and organization while Kairós has to do with change, exploration, discovery, innovation, intentions and dreams, and the emotions of young learners.

Agile and Adaptive Project Management

How Can These Methods Support Learning Projects?

In a previous chapter, the differences (few) and the commonalities (many) between business projects and school projects were reviewed.

Now, in order to make this comparison more comprehensive, it's necessary to explore a topic that since 2001, has been prompting an innovative evolution of the project management discipline—the so-called "agile" and "adaptive" approaches to project management.

The Agile Manifesto

As most PMs know, the wide dissemination of agile approaches such as Scrum, Kanban, and so on has been motivated by the need to overcome the limits of traditional project cycles in which scope, time, and cost need to be determined as early as possible. These are very problematic constraints in complex and rapidly changing environments such as software development for online platforms.

For this reason, a team of highly qualified and experienced project experts developed and signed the famous *Manifesto for Agile Software*

Development, written as contrasting priorities in managing adaptive projects compared to traditional prescriptive projects, which includes:

- People and personal interactions over processes and tools,
- Working software over comprehensive documentation,
- Customer collaboration over contract negotiations, and
- Responding to change over following an exact plan.

The preferences of the manifesto's authors were very clear, "While there is value in the second items in each line, we value the first ones more."

Moving to the educational context, schools are facing similar needs to overcome the limits of traditional teaching methods through a more student-centered learning approach focused on skills and practices that support the exploration of real-world challenges.

If we try to apply the *Manifesto for Agile Software Development* to the emerging trends in school systems, we can create a parallel comparison, as follows:

- Learners' needs *over* educators' prescribed programs,
- Real-world experiences *over* transferring facts and knowledge,
- Social collaboration learning *over* competitive individual achievement, and
- Assessments *for* and *as* learning *over* assessments *of* learning.

Subscribers of a potential *Manifesto for Project Based Learning* might agree, "While there is value in the second items in each line, we value the first ones more."

The 12 Principles of Agile Project Learning

The 17 authors of the *Manifesto for Agile Software Development* didn't confine themselves to a simple preference in four elements of evaluation. In fact, they shared a list of 12 principles as pillars of agile project approaches, such as the following three:

- Our highest priority is to satisfy the customer through early and continuous delivery of valuable software.

- Build projects around motivated individuals. Give them the environment and support they need, and trust them to get the job done.
- The best architectures, requirements, and designs emerge from self-organizing teams.

Carrying out the parallel exercise for education, we can imagine a similar *12 Principles for Agile Project Learning* that promote deeper learning and 21st century skills:

1. Our highest priority is to develop the potential of each learner as an active and effective designer and manager of her/his own learning projects.
2. Each learner needs strong social and emotional support to strive toward deeper levels of competency, expertise, and mastery across broad, interrelated sets of knowledge, skills, character qualities, and deeper learning strategies.
3. Learning projects need to focus first on students' own learning goals and personal interests, and then on the application of essential skills (especially the 4Cs) to developing wider and deeper knowledge and competencies.
4. Learners are best supported by a caring network of stable and supportive relationships with peers, adults, and community members.
5. Motivation is the fuel for learning. A supportive environment of co-learners, explorers, and mentors, with easy access to a wide variety of learning resources and tools, represent the passengers, devices, and vehicles of deeper learning.
6. Meta-learning—the reflection, evaluation, goal setting, planning, and managing of the learning processes—is essential to developing self-reliant, self-motivated, lifelong learners.
7. Making students' project work public by explaining, displaying, and presenting it to diverse audiences builds both essential learning and communicating skills and confidence.
8. Engaging in real-world projects offers students opportunities for deeper meaningful engagement and understanding, longer retention of lessons learned, and stronger motivation to embark on further learning journeys.

9. Learning technology tools free up time for deeper learning by taking care of rote learning tasks (such as information searching, organizing, and collaborative writing) and connect students to other learners and learning resources anywhere in the world.
10. Diverse learning environments that enable students to research online, quietly reflect, work in teams, experiment and create with powerful tools (such as those found in innovative Makerspaces), and present and exhibit their work, all support active, deeper learning.
11. The best projects, ideas, and solutions emerge from self-motivated, self-directed, self-organizing, highly collaborative, creative student teams.
12. Learning from errors and mistakes (best called "iterations") is essential to developing the competencies needed for success.

How Agile Methods Benefit Projects and Learning

After translating the principles of agile project management from the business environment to the world of education, it's now necessary to analyze why these principles are particularly effective when they are applied to learning projects.

The first reason is related to the educational mission of educators, which is to do all they can to develop all of their students' skills and competencies regardless of students' current level of accomplishment. Effective teachers see differing backgrounds, experiences, attitudes, and abilities as a positive benefit in helping students learn from one another and building empathy and respect for other people's unique gifts.

One critical success factor for all educators is "flexibility"—in this case, adapting new learning approaches (e.g., project based learning) to the needs of a single student or an entire class. Flexibility and adaptability—key qualities of proven agile practices and tools that can benefit the learning process because they enable teachers to:

- Ensure a progression of knowledge building and sense making with the progressive elaboration of a learning project's scope and plan,

- Generate emergent student project ideas and innovative solutions as the result of continuous team interactions and a rich exchange of collective knowledge sharing, and
- Maintain a healthy balance between "order and chaos" through a thoughtful mix of critical and creative thinking.

A second reason to favor the adoption of agile approaches in education is connected to the role that teachers play in supporting student learning projects.

Thanks to the growing number of successful experiences of project management volunteers in schools, many PMs can testify that the most successful project teachers were those who effectively played the role of project facilitator, mentor, and coach, and not the typical role of a directive, top-down project manager.

To be more precise, comparing the key roles in the agile world to expert project learning teachers, these teachers actually play roles similar to that of a Scrum Master, whose main duties are to:

- Create a cooperative environment in which project teams can be facilitated in their work of exploration, planning, and delivery;
- Enable teams' self-organizing by helping them define and share common project ground rules and make clear choices around communication methods and schedules;
- Act as a "servant leader" and "troubleshooter," able to catch early weak signals of potential problems and sensitize team members to dealing with solutions sooner than later; and
- Provide high visibility and sharing of project activities and results through the use of intuitive visual tools (don't forget that the school blackboard, now whiteboard and digital interactive whiteboard, is the ancestor of the project Kanban board).

The school may be the ideal environment to put the best agile methods and tools into practice through peer-to-peer collaborations between educators and project management practitioners. Through these sorts of collaboration, PMs will have opportunities to more deeply understand the power and effectiveness of agile methods and then use the lessons learned in these educational experiences in their everyday work environments.

Educators as Project Managers

How Can We Help Educators Become Better Project Managers?

> *I'm not sure how project managers can really help me.*
> *I didn't realize how many things in common*
> *I have with a project manager!*
> **—Two teacher responses to PMs as education mentors**

These two statements highlight the challenges for both educators and PMs to build the necessary bridges of understanding between their professions.

Here is how one project manager reflected on how the project-manager-to-educator bridge-building journey can unfold:

> *In 2006, when I started my journey into bringing project management into the school world, the most difficult obstacle to overcome was the seeming resistance of teachers toward my proposals to help them better manage learning projects with their students.*
>
> *In the beginning, there seemed to be a great deal of resistance to change on the part of the teachers, which I saw as a typical reaction of people who are dubious of the value of modifying their currently successful practices, working behaviors, and habits.*

It turned out that my first reactions were not correct.

I now know that most teachers are incredibly open-minded, constantly searching for new approaches to engaging and motivating their students.

Over time I realized that those initial hesitations were caused by my own resistance to accepting three fundamental assumptions about educators:

1. *A high percentage of teachers' efforts are dedicated to activities very close to those of project professionals working in the context of project, program, and portfolio management. We share a set of competences and skills much more similar than PMs would think, or teachers without project management mentors can realize.*

2. *Collaboration between project professionals and educators needs to be a "peer-to-peer" relationship in which each recognizes the need to learn from the other—PMs learning more about education, and educators learning more about project management—with the necessary time to translate and adopt parts of each other's working language, principles, processes, and culture.*

3. *Most significantly, teachers initially need help in providing project based learning experiences that give their students opportunities to hone the knowledge, skills and mindsets they need to be successful; teachers are not initially looking for help in managing projects for their students or themselves, as they are often not aware of just how the field of project management can help them.*

Having assisted more than 40 project based learning experiences in schools, now I can say that though the projects of the first years had some positive and promising results, I learned that the more I deeply understood the challenges of teaching and learning, the more valuable I became in helping teachers and their student projects be more successful learning experiences.

The biggest lesson I learned is that learning projects are so much more about the learning than the project results, and that teachers and PMs have extremely similar jobs with very different terms for very similar principles and practices.

Based on a wide variety of experiences of PMs working in the world's education systems, the following two sets of helpful advice are offered:

- First is a set of positive "virtues"—knowledge, understandings, and practices that most teachers and many students already have (but don't often see them as project management skills); PMs can leverage these developing project competencies to be more effective mentors for educators, students, and school administrators.
- Second is a set of negative, but avoidable, "sins" that PMs should be very aware of so that they can be more successful bridge-building mentors for educators and students.

Project Management Virtues That Teachers Most Likely Have Already

Yearly Planning

Among their many responsibilities, educators engage in two levels of yearly planning:

- The first level is where all teachers contribute to the planning of the entire school or district educational offerings for the year. It's an important planning process whose objective is to communicate the school and district goals and programs to their "customers"—parents, relatives of the students, the students themselves, and other community members; and
- The second level involves each teacher creating a plan for her/his students' educational activities and goals for the year. This plan must align with the guidelines established by the district, state, provincial, and national education authorities.

The visual planning tools that have been developed for the progressive elaboration of learning projects have been very useful for both teachers and administrators to communicate and motivate the updating of their planning documents as the inevitable changes occur during the school year.

Planning for Individual Needs

In addition to yearly planning, most educators develop personalized plans for individual students, particularly those students with special learning needs. The goal is to respect a key principle of most educational systems: to offer the same opportunities for learning and growth to each and every student.

These personal plans created by educators are very similar to a number of activities performed by professional project practitioners, including:

- The construction of alternative plans (e.g., contingency plans and fallback plans) to be activated in response to events that can affect a project either positively or negatively; and
- Planning for individual or collective professional training/ development events aimed at knowledge building or closing competency gaps and, as a consequence, improving project performance.

Communication Efforts

The similarity between the communication competences needed by educators and project professionals is even more evident and relevant.

As PMs know, the general rule of thumb is that some 70% of a project manager's time should be spent communicating with the project team and other stakeholders, both internal and external to the business organization.

It is reasonable to estimate that a teacher's time spent in communicating with students, parents, colleagues, school directors, and staff is easily above 90%.

Now, if communication is a key element to achieve the educator's mission, what are the main difficulties she or he must be able to overcome compared to a project professional?

There are three qualitative factors that make teacher communications with students more complex and delicate than communication with adults: Age, vocabulary, and digital fluency.

Age is undoubtedly the first factor. The same words or concepts expressed by a seven-year old child, compared to a 16-year-old or an adult, can have very different meanings. For example, take the word describing the third phase of the professional project cycle—*Execution*. Using this word with young students can easily conjure up a much darker and sinister meaning!

Language must adjust to the age-appropriate vocabulary of the students, and time must be spent to connect new terms with common experiences, metaphors, or existing vocabulary that students can use to understand a new term.

Also, if we consider that communication between students and adults can sometimes be between "digital natives" and older "digital immigrants," we can easily see how much a professional project practitioner can learn from an experienced educator (or even more from her/his digitally fluent students!) in terms of the style of communicating and explaining project methods or how to use online digital project tools, to a younger, digital-savvy generation!

Flexibility

Flexibility is one of most effective tools in a project manager's toolbox for coping with the uncertainty and mutability of many projects and programs.

Given the shifting nature of project activities, project practitioners and educators tend to respond in similar ways. Both try to adopt flexible measures aimed at making projects more adaptable to unexpected situations.

Educators are able to practice a very sophisticated level of flexibility. A good example of this occurred in a 2nd-grade learning project whose goal was to put on a stage show dedicated to classic and modern fairy tales. The teacher and students had decided to design and build a small theater with puppets inspired by the characters in famous fairy tales.

What was the unexpected event?

During the project development, the teacher discovered that pupils were using puppets to tell true stories inspired by their daily experiences with classmates, friends, parents, and so forth.

What was the flexible response of the teacher?

She simply abandoned the original idea of using classic fairy tales and transformed the puppet theater into a "drama laboratory" for students' daily life stories instead.

The resulting project had a highly positive, empathic, and emotional effect on students' parents and families that went way beyond all expectations.

What is the lesson learned from the use of "serendipity" to create even more impactful project results?

First, it teaches us that interactions within motivated and collaborative teams can generate ideas that might be more effective than those planned in the original *Project Charter*.

Second, we must face the fact that unanticipated shifts in the nature of project deliverables, even if not completed, can stimulate highly innovative solutions that are not easily anticipated by teachers or PMs.

More generally, it tells us that the adoption of flexible approaches is very often the best way to transform the uncertainty of project outcomes into a generator of new opportunities and even deeper learning.

This may be seen as "extreme" flexibility by some PMs, but in the right context, this approach to embracing uncertainty instead of simply fending it off by sticking to the original plan can have highly beneficial results and can show how much there is to learn from teachers challenged by highly diverse students to put flexibility and adaptability into everyday practice.

Attitudes Toward Errors

Another element of project virtues that educators likely possess is the constant attention they must dedicate to the emotional and relational dynamics within teams and toward other involved stakeholders.

As an extension of this "deeper flexibility" of educators, there is a related skill set that most teachers have developed: a positive attitude toward errors and mistakes.

One secondary school teacher, in response to a question concerning the ever-growing challenges of his profession, simply replied: "As teachers, we must invest in errors."

But the most interesting answer was prompted by a further question: "Why is it so difficult to deal with student mistakes?"

The teacher said that there are two categories of errors that are sometimes hard to differentiate, and can lead to two very different treatments and, as a consequence, two very different results.

The first category includes errors that result from a lack of attention or commitment and, more generally, from unproductive attitudes toward learning or to the immature behaviors of students.

In this first case, one effective response is to find a way to connect to some related interest or passion a student may have and use that motivation to increase the engagement and desire to learn beyond their mistakes—a highly challenging but critical approach to engaging each student in a way that makes learning a personal choice.

In the second category, where a student is motivated to learn but really doesn't understand the principle or process they are trying to learn, errors represent great opportunities to go further to discover why and how a different answer or design might be better. This often involves further developing one or more of the 4Cs skills:

- Critical thinking—an error can highlight a knowledge or skill "limit" that must be overcome for the student or group to improve the ability to analyze and answer a question, solve a problem, defend an issue, or clearly communicate the learning to others;
- Creative thinking—an error can represent a "window of opportunity" because it puts students face to face with an unexpected situation that, in turn, can give a motivational edge to the search for more innovative answers, solutions, positions, or perspectives; mistakes and errors can be viewed as just another "iteration" toward a better outcome;
- Communication—an error, if seen as a learning opportunity, can stimulate constructive communication exchanges with the teacher and other students, who can then play the role of mentor and coach of the student or group; and
- Collaboration—an individual error can also lead to a better understanding of the importance of collective action, where the multiple perspectives of a group can bring fresh approaches to deeper understanding and socially motivating ways to learn from mistakes.

PMs who have advised and mentored many teachers and student groups have often commented that without their peer-to-peer relationships with motivated educators, they would not have developed such a deep awareness of the positive and transformative power of mistakes.

Sharing of Experiences

There are some clear project virtues that both PMs and educators share, including:

- Each teacher is responsible for planning and delivering educational projects within a specific knowledge domain (math, literature, arts, etc.), with aspects of the projects managed in part, or entirely, by student teams;

- Teachers must integrate their educational projects into a coherent program of learning activities geared to the motivations of their students and the expectations of parents and school leaders, and the demands of the district, state, provincial, or national educational authorities (clearly lots of stakeholder expectations and a high need to share information and learning experiences!); and
- Teachers' projects and programs must be integrated into the portfolio of the educational offerings of the school or district.

Because coherence, consistency, and alignment along these three levels is essential, educators are frequently involved in planning meetings that demand intense exchanges of information about the work done, work in progress, and further work to be done.

Because frequent sharing of recent project experiences and lessons learned are essential for both educators and business PMs, as a project manager, it may be helpful for you to reflect on these questions:

- How frequent are retrospective meetings held where PMs have the time to share their current experiences, challenges, common problems, and issues?
- Are we confident as project professionals that the presence of a portfolio manager or a PMO (Project Management Office) representative is enough to ensure effective capitalization of the lessons learned by single-project managers?
- If we allocate an appropriate quantity of time to transform tacit knowledge into explicit knowledge, could we expect greater improvements in project performances?

As we have seen, when it comes to deep sharing of what works best (and not) in projects, business PMs can learn a great deal from educators.

Lifelong Professional Development

Society in the 21ˢᵗ century is demanding deep changes to the world of education—expansion and integration of cross-curricular learning, innovative teaching methods, intelligent use of new media, and so on.

The business world is living through a similar transformation process where project management needs to become more able to integrate scientific and humanistic disciplines.

Many studies of how complexity theory applies to projects are converging on the need to work across the boundaries of technical disciplines. In addition, new approaches are going beyond the limits of traditional project cycles as the best way to address the complexity and uncertainty of projects and programs in rapidly changing environments.

What could be the most effective tool that educators and project practitioners could both use to tackle these challenges?

This very question was asked of almost 100 teachers. The majority of them included the words *professional development* or *training* in their responses, together with some additional key qualities such as *lifelong*, *multi-disciplinary*, and *experience-based*.

Considering the three dimensions of the PMI "Talent Triangle"—technical project management, strategic and business management, and leadership—as a model for the professional growth of PMs, could a similar framework for the continuous development of an educator be appropriate?

One possibility for a parallel professional development model for the distinctive needs of educators could involve lifelong competency growth in:

- Diverse strategies to encourage students to develop wide and deep knowledge bases in specific subject disciplines or cross-disciplinary themes, corresponding to the technical project management dimension;
- The ability to constantly adapt and renew teaching methods in response to individual, social, and economic changes, corresponding to PMI's strategic and business management dimension; and
- The capacity to lead diverse students toward self-motivated and self-directed learning and to help develop the leadership capacity of all students, corresponding to the PMI leadership dimension.

It should be perfectly clear from all of the examples above that *educators are, in fact, practicing project managers, even though they may not know it yet!*

With so many virtuous similarities between the work of educators and the work of professional PMs, bridge building between education and project management should be a natural development once both sets of professionals find a common language; become aware of their differing perspectives, project vocabulary, and life experiences; and help one another to evolve a hybrid *"PM4Ed"* learning culture that leverages the best of both the worlds of educational project learning and business project management.

Sins Professional PMs Need to Avoid with Educators and Students

For all PMs who are able to avoid the following education "sins," a double reward is ensured: feeling proud of their positive contributions to the education world, and hearing teachers make comments such as:

> *I didn't realize how many things in common I have with project managers!*

Here are seven "Don'ts"—things PMs must strive not to do in educational settings so that their mentoring experiences will be much more successful and rewarding:

Don't Use Language That Is Too Technical or Business-Oriented

A project manager working with schools to introduce project practices in education told this story:

> *In 2006, at the beginning of my collaboration with a team of primary school teachers, I suggested starting with a common set of terms based on the business language of project management—* Project Charter, Work Breakdown Structure (WBS), Network Diagram, *status reports, etc.*
>
> *Very soon, thanks to the polite feedback of an expert teacher, I realized that this approach was just not going to work for primary school students (in retrospect, what was I thinking?).*
>
> *Her feedback was, "If we want to teach the project language to young learners (in this case, ages 6 to 11), it's better to use one of the most effective forms of communication with younger students—metaphors from their everyday experience.*

I started using "Project Identity Card" for Project Charter, *the* WBS *became the* "Project Tree", *the* Project Network chart *a* "Project Calendar", *and status reports transformed into* "Project Traffic Lights" *(red for* "stop —attention needed right away," *yellow for* "watch out," *and green for* "it's OK; keep on going"). *This worked much better and an evolving project management kit for primary students was born.*

What are the lessons learned from this story?
Adjust the language to the audience!
"WBS" is fine for middle and high school students, and *"Project Tree"* is appropriate for primary school students, with all levels of students understanding very similar basic concepts or principles in the terms that best relate to their levels of experience with project methods. As the number project experiences grow, so do students' abilities to absorb more complex concepts and more complicated methods.

Don't Explain "What" Concepts Without First Doing Some "How" Processes

Educators see learning projects as opportunities to embark on collaborative experiential journeys to explore new knowledge, answer important questions, devise solutions to problems, defend positions on issues with strong evidence, and convey one's deepest thoughts and feelings in artistic expressions. Learning projects are much more than slogs through a dictionary of unfamiliar project terms and concepts.

What is learned individually and in teams along the project learning journey is much more important than reaching the narrow destination of getting the project terminology just right, the documentation perfect, or having all the project results meet professional standards.

What does this mean for PMs working in educational settings?

The emphasis must be on having students learn project management methods from the experience of doing the project practices first, then reflecting on what was learned from these experiences in the students' own words. Introducing project concepts adapted to students' experience and language can then be done, as needed by the students.

As experience with learning projects grows and deepens over time, more "professional" project approaches and terms can be introduced, often as students tackle more ambitious projects that require a more refined understanding of effective practices that support more complex projects.

In short, *do first, reflect next, introduce project concepts and terms appropriate to the students' age and experience levels as needed, and then evolve toward professional project concepts and methods over time.*

Don't Be Too Critical in Evaluating Project Results

One of the first rules of providing effective feedback to students is to use the time-tested (and research-proven) language of "kind critiquing," which goes something like, "I really like how you did x and y, and I wonder if you did z if you might have a result you would like better."

Starting with multiple positive "I like" statements before introducing an "I wonder" improvement or alternative strategy provides students with confidence-building supports first, which enables them to better absorb different ideas or strategies that might work better in the future.

PMs in educational settings always need to remember that the learning outcomes are far more important than the quality of the project results or a strict adherence to professional project processes. Producing higher-quality results and applying project processes more faithfully happens gradually with experience as students develop their project skills.

Three qualities in working with students are extremely important: patience, a supportive attitude, and confidence that students will eventually and over time develop an internal desire to create higher-quality results and more effective and efficient processes. This, in turn, will drive their learning toward more professional project management approaches.

Learning is a gradual, developmental process that is driven by experiences that develop an internal need to know more and improve one's skills.

Don't Prescribe All Roles, Tasks, Timelines, etc., Leaving Little or No Student Choice

It may be somewhat appropriate with teachers and students who have never done a learning project before to start with a smaller, more prescribed project that follows more of a "recipe" approach. But experience has shown that even in introductory project experiences, both students and teachers need some freedom to exercise their creativity and individuality.

Student choice and "voice" are highly motivating aspects of learning that can more deeply engage students in project work and provide opportunities to "own" the goals and specific parts of the project. Giving students opportunities to choose their roles on a team, the tasks they will take on, chances to add their particular talents and ideas to the style and features of the product results, etc., can only increase the quality and depth of student learning.

As project learning experiences grow, so does the need for students to take more control of the entire project management processes, from defining the project to planning its course, doing the project work, and evaluating the outcomes.

The more project responsibilities students can manage, the more they can learn from their project experiences.

Don't Try to Support Excessive Numbers of School Projects—Quantity over Quality

From the experience of hundreds of professional PMs working with a wide variety of teachers and students in primary and secondary schools around the world, some helpful guidelines around quality interactions and mentoring have been learned, including:

- Mentoring a teacher for single student learning project can easily take 15–30 hours of time, and more if the project is ambitious;
- The more time a project management professional can spend learning about the students' and the teachers' needs and capacities, the higher the probability that the learning projects will be successful;
- Working with more than one teacher and their students and more than a single project at a time increases the probability that the quality of the mentoring will decline;
- The more teachers and student projects that PMs mentor over time (preferably one at a time), the more time they prefer to spend working with a single teacher to increase their depth of expertise in managing more and more complex projects with that teacher's students; and

- It can be very helpful to bring together a number of teachers who work with project manager mentors in a local geographic area to share their experiences and learn from one another; this can also stimulate other PMs who see the excitement and successes in applying project management to education to join in the fun!

When it comes to mentoring educators and students, quality always wins over quantity.

Don't Neglect the Review Phase's Celebrations, Presentations, and Recognitions

When students present their exemplary project work to the public in project fairs, project exhibitions, and formal presentations at conferences, they gain what may be the most valuable skills of all for their future success—the ability to articulately present to a large audience their ideas, experiences, and persuasive reasons why their work was so important to their learning and the beneficial impacts the project had on others.

Also valuable is the feedback the students receive from audience members during and after their presentations—how well their presentations are received and the kinds of questions and interest they get from audience members after the presentation is over.

Celebrating project success is also incredibly important to students. It gives them an opportunity to look back and feel proud of the contributions they made to the project and the things they learned. As part of the celebration, time should be set aside for each student to reflect on what was best about the project and what she/he would like to do differently in the next project to be even better project learners, managers, and leaders.

Formal or informal recognition of outstanding work done on the project is also a highly motivating experience for students. External recognition, if done thoughtfully and if it is appropriate to the value that each student brought to the project, can increase the desire to take on even more ambitious goals in the next project.

Take as much time as needed to have students present their project work, get feedback, celebrate successes, and be appropriately recognized for their contributions.

The Review (Closing) Phase may hold the most important learning experiences in the whole project!

Don't Avoid Spreading the Word to Other PMs on How Rewarding and Uplifting It Is to Be a Mentor

For all the reasons presented earlier in this book, it is extremely important to share your (positive) experiences with other PMs!

There is no reason to deprive your colleagues of the opportunity to join the growing numbers of PMs who are sharing their expertise with teachers and the next generations of students who will no doubt need deep project expertise to become lifelong learners, productive workers, caring family members, and actively engaged citizens.

There can be no greater pride in knowing that you've helped so many students become self-propelled learners, effective learning project managers, and more confident leaders.

And who knows? Maybe you'll be lending an important hand in helping to create the next generations of professional project managers who will lead the project management profession to new heights in managing and leading amazing projects that will uncover new answers to deep questions about our world and new solutions to our global challenges, take leading stands on issues of deep social significance, and create transforming works of artistic expression that move us all to understand ourselves and one another better, inspiring us to live more peacefully together.

That could turn out to be the best long-term project you've ever worked on!

The Future of Project Management in Education

Project Management as a Bridge to 21st Century Education

Conclusions to books, like the end of projects, are often two things at once – looking back from the end of one journey, and looking forward to the beginning of another.

Endings involve both rational and emotional reflections on past work done and the future work to come. And like good project reviews, they can be very personal, revealing sometimes difficult, and often deep, lessons learned.

These are Walter's personal concluding thoughts and feelings:

Thanks to the continuous reflections stimulated by the writing of this book, I have come to realize that my decade-long volunteering journey to bring project management to schools didn't start out with any clear destination in mind – only the desire to openly explore the education world and its relationships to the world of a project management practitioner like myself.

Since my belief is that organizations don't change until individuals do, my original goal wasn't to try to alter the world of education, but to change my own mindsets as to how a project manager might help students and teachers enjoy some of the same benefits I have experienced in my life as a project manager.

Surprisingly, this more "inner journey" has led me to ever more "outer" commitments.

At the conclusion of my current journey, I now have:

- *A deeper understanding of the core essence of project management, the project language and its uses, and the universality and interdisciplinary nature of projects*
- *A stronger appreciation of the beneficial effects that learning the project language and its practices can generate in the young minds of "digital native" learners*
- *A wider awareness of how project-based learning (PBL) is increasingly being practiced by teachers and students around the world, even though they may use different project language "dialects" and project methods, often without the benefit of a more universal, proven set of project principles and practices*
- *A clearer idea of how the project management profession can offer a universal language and essential practices that can (and does) help schools prepare all students for their present and future learning, work, family and community lives*

Those are just some of the most important lessons I learned from working with so many wonderful teachers and students on so many exciting projects.

As for the journey going forward, here are some of my new perspectives on the future of project management for education:

- *First, I have finally understood the final destination of the work I've been doing and the work now to be done, and that is:*

   The progressive and positive transformation of schools and education systems by adopting PBL best practices anchored in the best practices of Project Management, adapted to the needs of primary and secondary schools

- *Second, even with the many differences between education systems in various countries:*

   I believe the conditions are now right to begin integrating the project language and practices into all schools, *not just as disconnected "islands" of project learning as we've seen more of so far, but through wider and systematic initiatives supported by local or central educational institutions*

By this I don't mean we are facing a simple change that is easy and quickly achievable in the short term. What I really mean is that we are facing a window of opportunity for a profound change in education that will be increasingly supported by all stakeholders:

- *By* educators, *who are facing tsunamis of new information, with new knowledge to teach washing ashore in faster and faster waves – a context in which educators have only one option and one consequence: the option is to focus on the essential life skills that will never go out of fashion, such as creativity, collaboration and problem solving; the consequence is that project learning environments are the ideal context to develop and strengthen these skills*
- *By* students, *who are looking for school experiences that are more engaging, motivating, and yes, more fun (after all, learning is "wired-in" to be pleasurable, or we wouldn't have survived!) – in this context, the intensive use of projects that combine academics with solving real world challenges are powerful attractors and intrinsic motivators*
- *By* families, *who must assure a secure future for their children even though no one has a clue as to what the world will be like in even seven years' time – the only thing they can be sure of is that schools that offer their students real-life learning experiences, collaborative projects, multi-disciplinary and inter-disciplinary learning approaches, and the skills to become lifelong, self-motivated and self-directed learners, will likely have their students much better prepared for an uncertain and highly challenging future*
- *By* school administrators, *who are increasingly aware that like traditional factories created in the industrial revolution of 19th century, traditional schools have followed the same principles of top-down, one-size-fits-all mass production learning; at the same time, administrators are increasingly aware that their educational offerings must prepare all students for a future that demands bottom-up creativity, personalization, and*

self-motivated lifelong learners and doers, working together in meaningful learning projects

- By business leaders *competing within contexts of extraordinary unpredictability, who are looking for a workforce of creative thinkers, innovative problem solvers, people with strong communication and collaboration skills, and for expert project managers, team members and leaders*

- By governmental institutions, *who are facing increasing school drop-out rates (in Europe, currently an average of 14% of pupils quit before graduating from higher education) – the adoption of innovative and more engaging teaching approaches can be an important part of reversing this trend*

- By project managers *(this is my greatest hope), who will discover that the school environment is one of the most exciting places to grow both professionally and humanly, helping to create new generations of project-savvy learners and doers ready to tackle any problem needing a powerful project team to meet the challenge*

As indicated earlier, there are emotional realizations that are more difficult to explain that also contribute to the conclusions and beginnings of journeys.

For me, this realization is related to the recent untimely passing of a dear friend of mine, Giorgio Bensa, with whom I have shared the most inspiring and enriching moments of my ten-year journey to integrate project management into education.

Among the many volunteers I have had the good fortune of meeting and working with, Giorgio has been the one who has affected my values, my convictions and my commitment to change more than anyone else. And, above all, he has allowed me to more clearly see the true destination of our common educational journey and the route to follow in the next one.

As all giants who are able to see the future before others, Giorgio knew the real destination of our journey as project managers working in education. In 2012, during an interview captured in a video sponsored by the PMIEF, he stated:

> Someday project management will not be offered as an option, it will be considered like the alphabet, like the ABC's. That's the future.

The way forward to this future was very clear to Giorgio also, and it's contained in the phrase Giorgio typically used to inspire me and members of his volunteer teams working in schools. His mantra was, "Vietato dire: no se pol!" – a mix of Italian language and local dialect that can be translated into: "Never say: we can't!" – similar to the famous "Yes, we can" slogan, but in my opinion, much stronger and more immediately engaging.

With this precious legacy to always remember on my next exciting journey that has already started (hopefully spurred on by your reading of this book), I can finally close this last chapter with a positive message addressed to all project managers who would like to contribute to the construction of a solid bridge between education and project management, and between a concluding past and an emerging, more hopeful future:

Welcome aboard! Your project journey to a brighter future has just begun.

Project Bridges to 21st Century Learning

A Learning Project Sampler

This section features three real-life learning projects done in schools around the globe, where a professional project manager and a teacher (or teachers) worked together to provide 21st century learning experiences for students—bridges successfully built between education and project management!

The projects are sequenced by grade level—from youngest students to oldest, from elementary to middle to secondary school student projects—and feature the exemplary project methods used in each of the project cycle phases. (Some of these projects are also described in the PMIEF/P21 *Skills Map—Project Management for Learning*, available at http://www.p21.org/storage/documents/Skills%20Map/Project_Management_Skills_Map_Final.pdf)

The format for each project includes the following:

- *Project Intro—brief background "story" of the project*

- *Project Description*
  - ○ Project Goals
  - ○ Project Types (Inquiry, Design, Debate, Expression)
  - ○ Subject Areas (Language arts, Science, Arts and design, Technology skills, etc.)
  - ○ Related Career Pathways (Energy, Arts and media, Information technology, etc.)
- *Project Cycle Activities by Phase—*Define (Initiating), Plan (Planning), Do (Executing, Monitoring/Controlling), Review (Closing)
  - ○ Activities and Tools
  - ○ Project Work Examples
  - ○ 21st Century Skills Developed (see Project Learning Resources—21st Century Skills Descriptions in the Educator Guide, pages 90–97)

As a helpful summary reference guide to the project examples, a brief review of the key roles and project phases used in each of the projects is outlined in Project Learning Resources, Key Learning Components Review in the Educator Guide (green tabbed section), pages 82–87.

Primary Grade 2: Puppet Theater Project

PROJECT INTRO

Initial Drawings of the Puppet Theater

Students in a grade 2 class in Milan, Italy, were reading classical and modern fairy tales, answering questions and having discussions about the structure of the tales—characters, plot, conflicts, resolutions, moral of the stories, etc.

With the help of the art teacher and a project manager coach from a local PMI chapter, the students designed and created a puppet theater (shown to the right) to perform a puppet show based on their selections of fairy tales they thought would work best for a puppet show. They crafted the puppets, sets, props, etc.; practiced the show until they felt ready to present it to the public; and then organized and managed the public performance.

Primary Grade 2: Puppet Theater Project

PROJECT DESCRIPTION

Project Goals

- To read and hear a variety of classical and modern fairy tales, and answer critical thinking questions related to the tale's characters, plot, conflicts, resolutions, moral of the stories, etc.

- To choose a selection of fairy tales to put on as puppet shows, reflecting on why the chosen tales would be best for a puppet show

- To design and build a puppet theater and the puppets, props, scenery, etc., needed to perform the puppet tales

- To practice the performance of the puppet shows until ready to present to the public

- To plan and present a series of puppet shows to the public

Project Types

- Design
- Expression

Subject Areas

- Art and design
- Language arts
- Math

Related Career Pathways

- Arts and media
- Fashion design and manufacturing
- Engineering

Primary Grade 2: Puppet Theater Project

DEFINE (Initiating) PHASE

The project involved two teachers—a language arts and art teacher, one classroom of students, their parents and families, and a project coach from the local chapter of the Project Management Institute. The PMI Northern Italy Chapter also provided some funding for materials and expert help in constructing the puppet theater.

Brainstorming

Students visually brainstormed all the parts of the project as shown here:

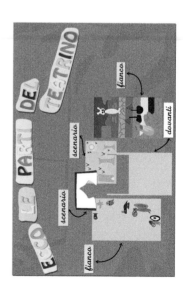

Mind Map

They then organized the parts of the project into similar functional clusters using sticky notes as shown here:

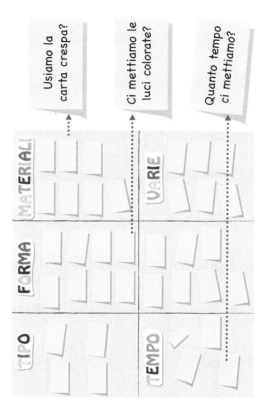

Primary Grade 2: Puppet Theater Project

PLAN (Planning) PHASE

The students created an **Activity Tree** containing a list of detailed tasks to be executed by the pupils with the support of the project coach and the supervision of the teacher.

Each activity was later turned into a **Project Calendar** in order to evaluate the progress of the project and provide any needed adjustments as shown here:

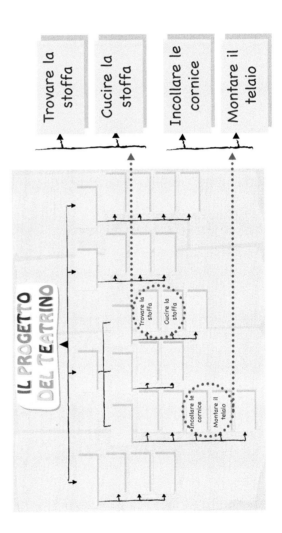

Primary Grade 2: Puppet Theater Project

DO (Executing & Monitoring/Controlling) PHASE

As the students progressed in carrying out each of the activities of the project they had the support of the coach from the PMI Northern Italy Chapter.

They regularly assigned a color (and happy, neutral, or sad faces) to a *Traffic Light Chart* that monitored the progress of important tasks. Adjustments were made, if necessary, to the Project Calendar and the resources needed — more student workers, more materials, more help, etc. — until that activity was back in the green light zone.

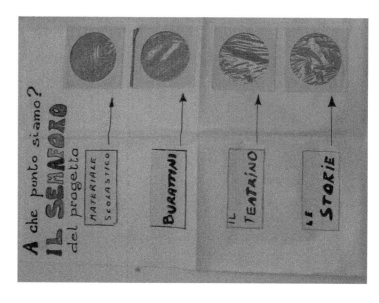

Traffic Light Chart Used by Students to Monitor and Control the Project

Primary Grade 2: Puppet Theater Project

REVIEW (Closing) PHASE

Each student created a "**Lessons Learned**" chart that answered the following questions:

- What new things did I learn?
- What was the most difficult thing?
- What was the most enjoyable part?
- What would I change for the next time?
- What could I have done better?

This led to sharing each of the students' *Lessons Learned* charts and some additional reflections, as well as a party celebration for a project well done!

Here is a photo of the final project celebration and an actual performance:

Final Performance of the Puppet Theater

67

Middle Grade 7: Water Makes . . . a School! Project

PROJECT INTRO

The participants in this project were the students of a middle school located in Matera, a very ancient city in Southern Italy. Their idea was conceived on the banks of the Gravina Creek, among erosive furrows 70–80 meters deep and within a beautiful canyon full of meanders, lateral tributaries, terraced walls, artistic pinnacles, and suspended valleys.

Right there, they realized that the history of their land was also a human history, the story of a community of the Neolithic age that was able to survive in very difficult conditions thanks to the ability to exploit the limited resources in their environment.

In fact, after creating brilliant solutions to their housing problem, these ancestors were faced with yet another challenge: the lack of water. Thanks to their extraordinary ingenuity, they were able to find the best solutions for collecting and delivering water through wells and tanks, locally called *palombari*.

Excited by these fantastic discoveries of the ancient history of their city, the students went back in the classroom

with a very clear objective—to become the guardians of the natural element that sustained their ancestors and their lives. Together with their teachers, they decided to launch a school project named "Water Makes . . . a School!"

Here is the poster they created outlining the project details in a *Project Identity* chart:

Middle Grade 7: Water Makes . . . a School! Project

PROJECT DESCRIPTION

Project Goals

- To increase the students' awareness about the importance of knowing their environment, its story, and its culture
- To increase the students' sense of responsibility about the need to protect the environment and artistic heritage

Project Types

- Design
- Expression

Subject Areas

- Art and design
- Language arts
- History

Related Career Pathways

- Arts and media
- Building and environmental design
- Energy
- Engineering
- Health science

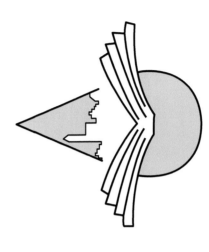

This is the project logo the students created

Middle Grade 7: Water Makes . . . a School! Project

DEFINE (Initiating) PHASE

After the construction of the *Project Identity Card*, a collective *Brainstorming* session elicited the many details of the students' initial dreams for the project, which became clearer and more engaging during their discussions.

To better interpret their role as guardians of the treasures of their city, each student imagined being one of the ancestors of the city who came to visit their classroom and what that ancestor would be astonished to find and what was lacking in their modern school. Many project ideas were discussed and shared before starting the final selection from a big poster that seemed to explode with sticky notes representing different ideas.

In the next step, the creative energy unleashed from the brainstorming was focused on creating a detailed *Mind Map* in which students were able to bring order to their "storm of ideas." At the completion of this phase, the students' *Mind Map* was, in fact, a beautiful illustration of the first steps of the project, and they realized that the next phases of *Planning, Execution,* and *Closure* would now be much easier.

Here are the *Brainstorming* and *Mind Mapping* charts the students created:

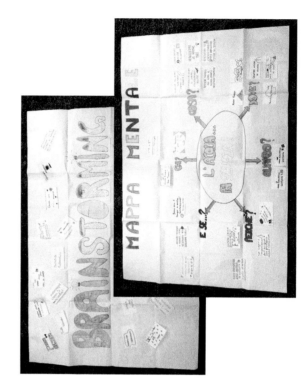

PLAN (Planning) PHASE

Thanks to the information visualized in the *Mind Map*, in particular within the "what" branch, the construction of the *Activity Tree* was quite simple and quick.

Then, thanks to the facilitation and supervision of the teacher, the students put each task on a monthly *Project Calendar* by taking into account the needed sequence of activities as shown here.

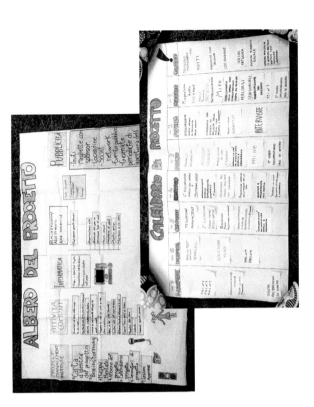

Middle Grade 7: Water Makes . . . a School! Project

DO (Executing & Monitoring/Controlling) PHASE

A View of the "Palombara Lungo" Visited by the Classroom During the School Project

The *Executing Phase* generated deeply engaging moments in which the students felt like both the ancestors and modern-day inhabitants of their city.

In particular, the teacher made sure that both the whole class and each individual student achieved their learning goals through a careful balance between individual and collective experiences and reflections.

No one was excluded because, as the teacher said, "The students are like a puzzle in which each tile is essential to create the expected results and achieve the project goals."

The most exciting experience for students in their journey to learn the history of their land, was the visit to the "Palombara Lungo" (see image to the right), an ancient and majestic water tank named "the Water Cathedral" that is located under the city of Matera, one the most ancient UNESCO World Heritage Sites.

REVIEW (Closing) PHASE

The use of the *Project Traffic Lights* was very helpful to continually check in on the progress of the eight-month project as shown below.

In reviewing the project, two choices stood out as major contributors to the success of the project:

- The choice of grouping all the activities in relation to the basic project cycle phases in the project management methodology. In this way, students and teachers had the opportunity to evaluate the impacts of each phase and the overall project in a structured way; and

- The choice of grouping all the efforts not related to specific project cycle deliverables into a specific domain called "common activities." In this way, both students and teachers had the opportunity to realize the how the ongoing project monitoring and control contributed to the success of the project.

Secondary Grade 11: Nuclear Energy—Friend or Foe? Project

PROJECT INTRO

Students in an 11th-grade chemistry class in Medford, Oregon, studied the pros and cons of nuclear energy as a viable and secure energy source for the future.

After studying the three principal types of radiation and performing a lab in measuring different forms of energy (as shown above), student teams were challenged to make the case for or against the use of nuclear energy.

Students presented their positions in a set of PowerPoint slides, offering the most convincing evidence they accumulated in their research to support their argument.

A lively discussion and debate on the issues followed.

Students and Teacher Discussing the Pros and Cons of Nuclear Energy

Secondary Grade 11: Nuclear Energy—Friend or Foe? Project

PROJECT DESCRIPTION

Project Goals

- To understand the three principal types of radiation and their benefits and risks to society
- To measure a variety of forms of energy and get a sense of the amount of energy produced by various generation methods, especially nuclear power
- To research the scientific, historical, social, political, military, health, and global aspects of nuclear energy
- To form position on the use of nuclear energy for the future and support this position with the most convincing evidence possible
- To respectfully debate the issue of nuclear power, weighing the evidence, considering different points of views, and engaging in a balanced discussion of the pros and cons

Project Types

- Debate
- Inquiry
- Design

Subject Areas

- Science—chemistry, physics
- Math
- Social studies
- Language arts
- Information technology

Related Career Pathways

- Energy
- Information technology
- Health science

Secondary Grade 11: Nuclear Energy—Friend or Foe? Project

DEFINE (Initiating) PHASE

For interdisciplinary projects like this nuclear energy project, the teacher follows the school's curriculum map (shown below), which outlines the learning objectives and main curricular activities that are suggested for the combination of subject areas—in this case, science and social studies—in a "Chemistry in the Community" theme.

The driving question in this project was: "Can nuclear energy be a viable and secure energy source for the future?"

The students formed project teams, performed experiments, and did research as part of the curriculum activities guided by the teacher. Each project team took a position on the issue, based on their research findings, and then built a strong case with convincing scientific and historical evidence for their position on the issue.

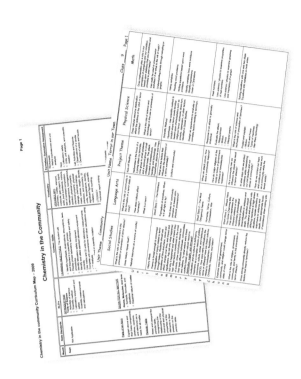

Curriculum Map – South Medford High School Uses Curriculum Mapping to Integrate Instruction Across Subject Areas.

Secondary Grade 11: Nuclear Energy—Friend or Foe? Project

PLAN (Planning) PHASE

From their work on hands-on lab projects, recorded in their energy labs notebooks, and from their research on nuclear energy, captured in the *Research Findings* documents, the different project teams decided on the position they would take and the further research they needed to bolster the case for their position (key chemistry principles like those shown below were very important to the defense of their positions).

Each team self-defined the roles for each of its members, identified the research sources they would explore, and set timelines for when each part of the project would be completed.

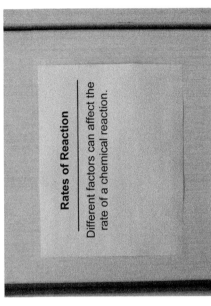

Rates of Reaction

Different factors can affect the rate of a chemical reaction.

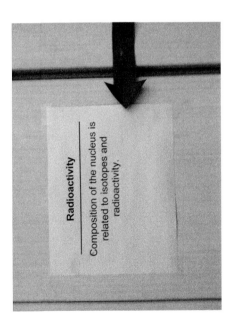

Radioactivity

Composition of the nucleus is related to isotopes and radioactivity.

Student Artifacts from Nuclear Energy Project

Secondary Grade 11: Nuclear Energy—Friend or Foe? Project

DO (Executing & Monitoring/Controlling) PHASE

Students Discussing the Project Issues and the Evidence

The teacher provided a number of provocative *Issue Questions* to stimulate critical thinking and to motivate deeper research on the various positions the student teams were taking. Examples of these questions included:

- Would you provide nuclear power plants to Saudi Arabia or another Middle Eastern country?
- What would a country need to do to convert a nuclear power plant into a weapon?

Students then created a *Presentation Outline* and a set of PowerPoint slides that provided the best evidence from their research to support their position on the nuclear energy issue.

Secondary Grade 11: Nuclear Energy—Friend or Foe? Project

REVIEW (Closing) PHASE

Students Working on Their Lab Exercises to Better Understand What Radiation Really Is

After the project was over, the students and teacher held a *Review Session* on how well the project went and what was learned from managing and leading such a controversial, issues-based project. Some of the questions discussed were:

- Were project goals met and the end result completed on time?
- Were the resources and research support adequate?
- Were the right roles assigned for each team member and did those team members perform well?
- Were outside experts, advisors, or information sources used well?
- Was team communication effective?
- Were team decisions made well?
- Were project changes handled well?
- Were disagreements resolved well?
- What were the most significant achievements, individually and group?
- What would make an even better project next time?
- What were the most important lessons learned?

Life Skills Project Terms	Learning Project Terms	Career/Professional Project Terms	Career/Professional Project Terms Definitions
Team	Project Participants (Champion, Manager, Team Members, Advisor/ Coach, Evaluator, etc.)	Stakeholder	An individual, group, or organization who may affect, be affected by, or perceive itself to be affected by a decision, activity, or outcome of a project, program, portfolio.
	Risk	Threat	A risk that would have a negative effect on one or more project objectives.
Plan	Work Plan	Work Breakdown Structure	A hierarchical decomposition of the total scope of work to be carried out by the project team to accomplish the project objectives and create the required deliverables.
Group of Steps	Group of Tasks	Work Package	The work defined at the lowest level of the work breakdown structure for which cost and duration can be estimated and managed.
Workaround	Workaround	Workaround	A response to a threat that has occurred, for which a prior response had not been planned or was not effective.

113

PROJECT MANAGEMENT
FOR EDUCATION

THE BRIDGE TO 21ST CENTURY LEARNING

Project Learning Guide for Educators

By Bernie Trilling and Walter Ginevri

Library of Congress Cataloging-in-Publication Data has been applied for.

ISBN: 978-1-62825-457-0

Published by: Project Management Institute, Inc.
    14 Campus Boulevard
    Newtown Square, Pennsylvania 19073-3299 USA
    Phone: +1-610-356-4600
    Fax: +610-356-4647
    Email: customercare@pmi.org
    Internet: www.PMI.org

Book cover designed by: Andrea Staricco

Table of Contents

Educator Foreword

by Jim Snyder, PMI Founder and Lifetime Innovator

As one of the founders of the Project Management Institute (PMI) back in the 1960s, I have long held a strong opinion that the only way for project management to reach its full potential in driving solutions to world problems was to create a generation of project-oriented people to solve project-oriented problems. The only way to achieve that objective would be to fully integrate project management skills into our K–12 educational programs. That means we must first have project-oriented educators—and this might be just a small problem! After all, business/industry and education are two very different worlds.

Project management is not rocket science, although there might not have been any rocket science without it! Project management—all that "stuff" that goes into the successful planning, organizing, executing, and delivery of successful project-oriented work—has become part of our everyday lives, and we acquire these skills in a very different way from most of our other life skills.

Like it or not, we have evolved to the point where most of our productive work takes the form of a project. Life is a series of continuing, overlapping, and interrelated projects. "Projects" are the way we get things done. Unlike many other skills, managing these various projects is important to our professional, social, and daily lives. The way we manage projects is not so very different from one environment to another, but we may acquire the skills we need to manage projects from very different sources.

Many of us had our first introduction to the world of project management in our professional lives when we found ourselves responsible for a major project. For many, it was an unexpected career change! We needed to learn quickly how to handle ourselves in the ever-changing and ever more complex world of projects. Our learning and knowledge base grew from our experiences in engineering, heavy construction, pharmaceuticals, aerospace, the military, and the oil and gas industries. The industrial acceptance and implementation of project management principles

and practices soon spread to an ever-widening group of businesses and industries. Today, project management is a part of almost everything we do.

From the original industrial/business base, PMI developed *A Guide to the Project Management Body of Knowledge (PMBOK® Guide)*, which set the language for engineering and business project management. And now, providers of project management training, education, and consulting are available, worldwide, to the engineering and business communities based on the language, processes, and practices that have developed from the early 1960s. This has become the language of professional project management.

But what about those other environments, such as education, our social lives, and our daily activities in which managing project-oriented work is just as important? A 2006 report by the Partnership for 21ˢᵗ Century Skills found the U.S. workforce "ill-prepared for the demands of today's (and tomorrow's) workplace." Lacking were both basic skills and applied skills such as critical thinking, problem solving, oral communications, teamwork, leadership, and others—all components of the project management process. Studies like this one and others focused educators' attention on project based learning (PBL), developed by the Buck Institute for Education and many others. PBL is a teaching method that engages students in learning through participation in interdisciplinary projects. As the process and implementation of PBL continued to grow and became accepted by more and more educators in the late 1990s, it took on a language of its own.

Civic and community organizations, as well as governmental groups, have begun to use project management processes to meet the demands of 21ˢᵗ century project-oriented work. Project based learning educational programs are starting to reach into classrooms far down through the K–12 structure, universities are making project management courses of study from the Bachelor to PhD levels available to students of all ages, and industrial/business segments such as information technology are requiring project management skills, including agile project management training, for their professionals. With the explosion of interest and the application of new processes to manage project-oriented work, it was inevitable that the two project-related cultures would eventually meet. And now they have.

If it looks like a project, acts like a project, and has all the characteristics of a project, then it must be a project! If we manage it like a

project, does it really matter what we call the processes we use? But the differences are not all in the language alone. Educators take a different approach to problem definition from that which might be taken by an engineer. There is little difference in the processes used by both communities; however, the emphasis and definition of these processes varies in the two communities. Confusions arise when the engineer and the educator try to collaborate on a research project or when a new business-oriented project manager joins an educational project team well-versed in PBL learning methods. Misunderstandings often result, reducing the efficiency and the effectiveness of the project teams. If only there were a way for these two communities to share their processes and learning without the possibility of confusion or misunderstandings.

In 2006 and 2007, the two communities made an effort to agree on common terminology and to bring their project processes together in a more unified approach. Some progress was made. However, no lasting agreements or translations from business to education terminology were fully developed. During the past few years, both the approaches to managing project-oriented work based in the professional (business/ industrial) world and in the educational system have grown and matured.

The language and process differences between the way project-oriented work is understood in the world of business and in the world of education have continued to be ironed out. An understanding of the differences between these two worlds has become more important as managing projects becomes a true learning and life skill that impacts every aspect of our personal, social, and professional lives.

In the early days of project management, our concerns were to establish the processes and create a knowledge base for a new profession. And over the years, we have done that. However, it is no longer acceptable for the profession to rely on on-the-job learning as the major educational source for those undertaking responsibility for major projects. Future project managers must come to the job with the tools and skills they need. This can only be accomplished if project management becomes a major life skill taught as one of the basic tools needed to manage the projects of learning, work, and life. I believe the teaching of the basic and applied skills identified by the Partnership for 21st Century Skills back in 2006 must become a reality if we hope to meet the challenges of this century. Some progress has been made, but until we have fully integrated project management and project based learning into the K–12 curriculum, the job will not be done. Giving project managers and

educators a better understanding of each other's viewpoints will go a long way toward making this needed integration a reality.

Walter Ginevri and Bernie Trilling have unique talents that allow them to address the issues of process and language differences that exist between project management and education. They both have experience in the world of education and in the world of business project management, and they have been acutely aware of the need for bringing the two worlds together for many years. This book aims to bridge these language and cultural barriers and empower both project management professionals and educators with the skills they need to bring their combined talents to bear on 21ˢᵗ century challenges.

The unique "flip" format of the book allows a quick change in perspective from educator to project manager and highlights the similarities as well as the differences in project processes and terminology. I think you will find this book a great step forward in support of the evolving transformation of education to meet our global, local, and business/education challenges. Use it to broaden your understanding of the management of life's projects: professional, business, social, or educational. Most of all, have some fun while learning to value and learn from the viewpoints of others—a much needed collaborative skill that will no doubt lead to a better world through all our learning, work and life projects to come!

James R. Snyder
Founder
Project Management Institute

Educator Preface

A "Two-Books-in-One" Overview

The book you are holding, *Project Management for Education* (*"PM4Ed"* for short), is actually two books in one: an *Educator Guide* and a *Project Manager Guide* to bringing the advantages and benefits of project management's powerful and practical principles and practices to the world of education.

By flipping this book over, you can switch between the two guides to explore how both educators and project managers (PMs) are increasingly moving toward the same goal—to help all students become more successful 21st century learners, well prepared for future work, citizenship, family, and community life.

PM4Ed aims to help build indispensable bridges between project management and education, to support the evolving transformation of education to equip students with the essential skills to tackle our world's "glocal" (global and local) problems, and to empower all learners to successfully manage their personal, social, and life challenges.

The *Project Learning Guide for Educators* (the side of the book you are now reading) introduces education-friendly versions of the tried-and-true project success strategies that expert project managers have refined over lifetimes of study and practice.

It is presented in seven Educator Chapters:

1. Bringing Project Management into Classrooms and Homes
2. Project Management as Learning, Work, and Life Skills
3. Project Based Learning (PBL) and Project Management (PM)
4. The Timeless Time Management Challenge
5. Agile and Adaptive Learning Project Methods
6. Evaluating Projects—Products, Process, and Learning Progress
7. The Future of Project Management in Education

This is followed by the center rainbow-colored "bridge" section of the book (shared by both the Educator and Project Manager guides), which includes Project Bridges to 21ˢᵗ Century Learning, a series of illustrated examples of real-life learning projects carried out in primary through secondary classrooms and communities around the world. These authentic case studies of successful learning projects highlight the 21ˢᵗ century competencies students developed and the project learning strategies they used. They also demonstrate how educators and professional project managers can work together to help all students and teachers become more powerful project learners and leaders.

Also in this center bridge section is the Project Learning Resources materials, which offer a wide variety of supporting resources and tools for both educators and project managers, including project learning pathways, a project learning research summary, a 21ˢᵗ century skills framework description, a learning project methods comparison table, a project management for education glossary, and lists of helpful books, online resources, and more.

If you flip the book over, you will be able to explore the *Project Learning Guide for Project Managers,* which offers a concise roadmap for adapting business-related project management expertise to the learning needs of teachers and students, bringing the power of proven project methods to education, and motivating student learning in rainbows of diverse projects across the globe.

With the support of the Project Management Institute Educational Foundation (PMIEF), project management principles and practices throughout both guides have been "translated" from the technical project language of business and engineering and adapted to fit the common vocabularies of teachers and students working on learning projects in everyday classrooms.

Educator Author Page

Bernie Trilling

*Well-managed learning projects can be some
of the sturdiest bridges to a brighter future.*

Around 2005 I had the good fortune to meet Jim Snyder, one of the inspirational founders of the Project Management Institute. A born innovator, Jim was once again looking into his trusty crystal ball and in it he saw ever so clearly that unless project approaches were cultivated early in schools, both the future pipeline into the project management profession, and the skills increasingly required for success in future learning, work and life, would be sadly lacking.

His vision of well-managed learning projects happening regularly in schools around the world, readying students for the project world that was rapidly emerging, was inspiring and deeply resonated with my own ideas on transforming learning for the 21st century.

Back then project based learning (PBL) was just starting to catch on in a big way in education, thanks to the efforts of the Buck Institute for Education and many others. I also saw that if PBL was to really take hold, it would need the expert wisdom of a profession built on a long history of what it really takes to have successful projects.

But there was one catch—for PBL to adopt project management methods, a "translation" of technical business-based project management language and concepts was needed before all that expertise and those deep treasure troves of hard-earned project wisdom could be adopted for use in classrooms and schools.

With the support of PMI's Educational Foundation (PMIEF), and their extraordinarily supportive staff members like Diane Fromm who enthusiastically shared this vision, I managed to cajole a number of organizations into coming together to discuss this great opportunity to fill in a missing gap in the PBL movement. Thus, an early "Project Learning

Partnership" was formed, as illustrated in this excerpt from a 2006 PMIEF online article:

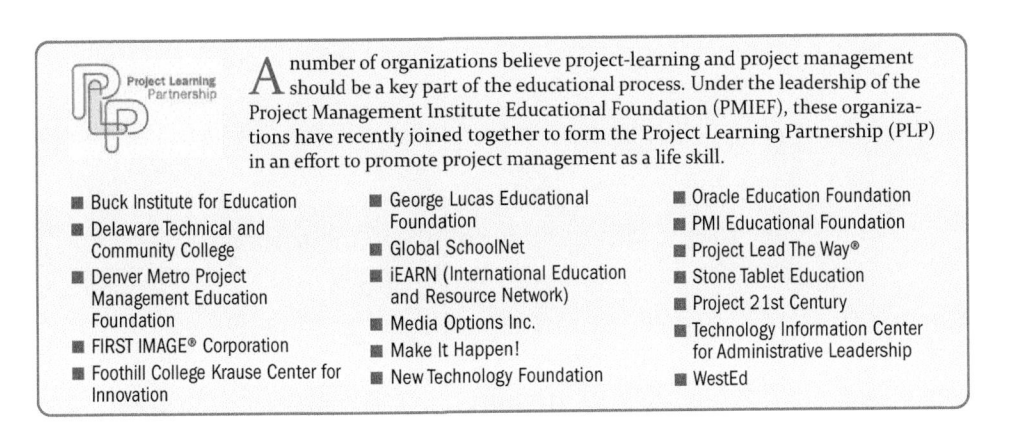

A number of organizations believe project-learning and project management should be a key part of the educational process. Under the leadership of the Project Management Institute Educational Foundation (PMIEF), these organizations have recently joined together to form the Project Learning Partnership (PLP) in an effort to promote project management as a life skill.

- Buck Institute for Education
- Delaware Technical and Community College
- Denver Metro Project Management Education Foundation
- FIRST IMAGE® Corporation
- Foothill College Krause Center for Innovation

- George Lucas Educational Foundation
- Global SchoolNet
- iEARN (International Education and Resource Network)
- Media Options Inc.
- Make It Happen!
- New Technology Foundation

- Oracle Education Foundation
- PMI Educational Foundation
- Project Lead The Way®
- Stone Tablet Education
- Project 21st Century
- Technology Information Center for Administrative Leadership
- WestEd

This early attempt to rally forces behind the integration of PBL and project management accomplished some groundbreaking work, but it wasn't until a number of years later when support within both PMI and PMIEF grew for this initiative (thanks to the exemplary work done in schools from pioneering PMI project managers like Walter Ginevri, the co-author of this book) that things began to really take off.

Now looking back from 2017, PMIEF has made incredible strides in paving the way for educators to really embrace the integration of PBL and project management. As an added bonus, both teachers and education administrators are increasingly adopting project management principles and practices for managing one of the most complex and important social institutions that exist in virtually every village, town, city and region – their local schools and educational institutions.

As you will see in this "2-in-1" book, many bridges and collaborations are now in place and growing strong, with many new bridges under construction and older ones being remodeled and scaled-up:

- The early Project Learning Partnership (PLP) has grown into the Project Learning Network (PLN) with over 30 active member organizations spanning the world of engaging learning projects for students
- PMIEF now offers a plethora of free learning materials, toolkits, guides, skills maps, badging micro-credentials, video case studies, professional development opportunities, and much more on its website—https://www.pmief.org/

- Schools, districts, regions, states and countries now have a wide variety of exciting project management for education learning initiatives in place and growing
- Career and technical education programs are rapidly adopting project management as a core competency across many career clusters, especially those preparing students for the important STEM jobs of the future
- PMIEF continues to sponsor motivating scholarships for students interested in pursuing project management as a profession
- And so much more!

This book is yet one more bridge-building effort, connecting both Educators and PMs in their common desire to see every student benefit from the skills, understandings and mindsets that the integration of project management and project based learning offers.

And after all, as you will also discover in this book, *well-managed learning projects can be some of the sturdiest bridges to a brighter future that we can all build together.*

This book is dedicated to all students everywhere who, with the caring support of parents, teachers, and their communities, will become the self-propelled, empowered, lifelong learners and doers who will build that brighter future.

Educator Introduction

What Does Project Management Bring to Education?

> *If we teach today's students as we taught yesterday's,*
> *we rob them of tomorrow.*
> **—John Dewey**

We live in a sea of accelerating change.

In every corner of our world, education is striving to meet society's rapidly shifting demands for new knowledge, deeper skills, and higher levels of competence. What students now need to succeed in learning, work, family, and civic life is dramatically different from what was needed when their parents were in primary school.

Connected digital tools such as smartphones, tablets, and laptops instantly link us to vast global libraries of internet media, and help make the sometimes tedious tasks of learning and creating easier, quicker, better, and more fun. As a result, we now can shift our attention to mastering more complex (and quintessentially human) skills such as *critical and creative thinking, problem solving, effective communicating, collaborating, self-motivation, persistence*, and a lifelong passion for *self-directed learning*. These essential 21st century skills and mindsets are rapidly rising to the top of many nations' lists of priority education goals for all students.

Project based learning (PBL), a set of engaging and powerful learning methods organized around motivating projects, is providing more and more students with new opportunities to exercise and develop these essential competencies, and PBL is quickly becoming a common TLA (three-letter acronym) for the learning approach most desired in modernizing education systems. As educators everywhere adopt more project-oriented learning methods in their classrooms, schools, and community programs, new questions arise, and more teachers (along with their students, parents, and administrators) are asking:

> *How do we manage all these learning projects, and how can I help students be more effective designers and managers of their own learning?*

What a perfect question for the project management profession to help answer!

And what an incredible opportunity for project managers, teachers, and students everywhere to collaborate on well-managed projects that enhance the learning capacity of countless learners, educators, and parents; bring powerful educational and social benefits to society; and inspire work toward a better future, rich with all sorts of exciting and beneficial projects.

The Five Ps of Project Management for Education

I feel like every project I work on is a dream project,
so long as I am learning.
—**Simeon Kondev**

There are many versions of lists of the key qualities of project management that often start with the letter P. Five of these "P-words" seem to best capture the essence of the mindsets and methods most central to adapting professional project management to the learning and teaching needs of students and educators, as illustrated here:

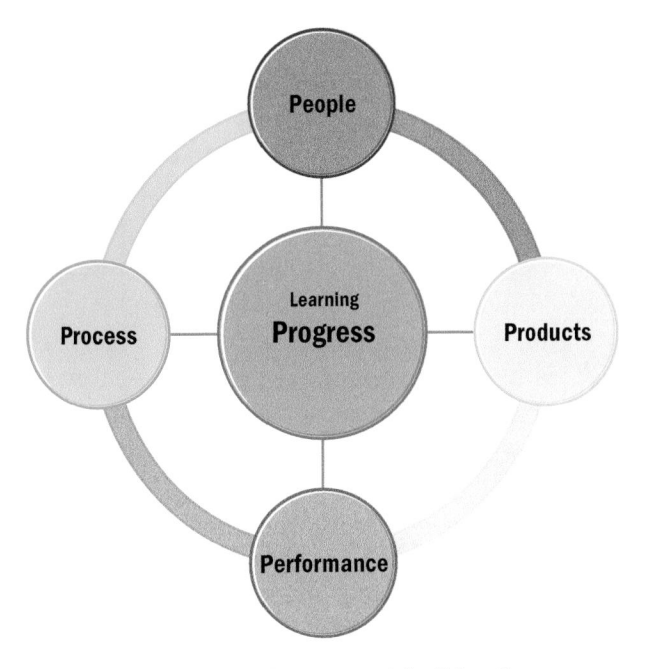

The 5Ps of Project Management for Education

The following is a brief outline of the most essential project practices in each of the 5P categories as an advance organizer and a "preview of coming attractions" that will be explored in greater detail in the rest of the book:

- *People*—*manage motivations, interactions, and teamwork*
  - Gain commitment of team members to the project goal
  - Manage the expectations of all project stakeholders
  - Communicate clearly and frequently with all project players
  - Collaborate productively and respectfully with all project members
  - Solve problems using effective critical and creative thinking

- *Process*—*apply proven project management strategies*
  - Follow best practices in each of the project cycle phases:
    - *Define* (Initiating)
    - *Plan* (Planning)
    - *Do* (Executing & Monitoring/Controlling)
    - *Review* (Closing)
  - Create a clear *Project Definition*
  - Commit to following the collaborative decisions in the *Teamwork Agreement*
  - Create, follow, and update changes in the project *Work Plan*
  - Hold regular *Check-in Meetings* and record all updates and project changes
  - Evaluate and record progress during and at the close of a project for *Product* results, *Process* quality, and learning *Progress*

- *Products*—*create high-quality project work with strong impacts*
  - Keep overall quality and craftsmanship of the project results as high as possible
  - Make sure project goals are achieved and the results are effective and useful

○ Seek feedback from the intended audience to ensure that expectations have been met, with ideas for future improvements

- **Performance**—*effectively manage the project process, product, and teamwork*
  ○ Ensure that the goals of the project are met
  ○ Effectively manage all phases of the project cycle
  ○ Meet all schedules and timelines
  ○ Use all resources, tools, and materials productively and efficiently
  ○ Effectively guide the implementation of all project updates and changes
  ○ Respect the motivations and expectations of project members and stakeholders

And most important for applying project management methods to education, a focus on:

- **Progress** in learning—*deepen and broaden the learning gains for both students and educators*
  ○ Track and celebrate gains in knowledge and expertise
  ○ Recognize increases in skills and project performance
  ○ Share reflections on growth in character qualities and motivation
  ○ Honor competency gains in the ability to reflect, revise, and plan further projects

There is an important difference between learning projects and most business projects, where the emphasis is often on being on time, on budget, and delivering exactly what is intended. In education, even if a project is not fully completed or takes longer than expected, and even if it uses more resources than expected, as long as the learning gains are truly significant for both individuals and project teams, the project may be considered worthy and successful. Always remember:

The learning gains from educational projects are the most important results!

Project management is the art of making things happen.
—J. D. Meier

Bringing Project Management into Classrooms and Homes

Why Is Project Management So Important to Student Success?

As you will learn in this book, project management is not just a set of principles and practices used exclusively by professional businesses in complex, large-scale engineering or product development projects (like a NASA mission to Jupiter, building a highway bridge, or designing a new digital device).

The core concepts and methods of the project management profession can be adapted to all kinds of projects, including:

- Everyday life projects:
  - Cooking a holiday meal
  - Planning and planting a garden
- Learning and school projects:
  - Developing a science fair exhibit
  - Performing a play
- Community projects:
  - Implementing a home energy savings program
  - Creating services for the homeless

Projects are used in practically every occupation and human pursuit imaginable. *Projects have become a basic unit of work and life in the 21st century.*

Likewise, *learning projects are becoming a basic unit of instruction and learning in the 21ˢᵗ century.*

Students, teachers, community educators, and parents (who are a child's first and everlasting teachers) can all benefit greatly from applying the simple yet powerful ideas and effective strategies used by the best professional project managers.

What's in It for Students?

*I always ask the question, "How can
I apply this in the real world?"
Project management has made my confidence grow,
and if I can do it in this class, I can do it out there.*
—**High school student**

Students today need more opportunities to develop the skills, understandings, and mindsets that will help them be successful in school, at work, and in their daily lives. Learning through projects, or project based learning (PBL), offers students ways to develop the "4Cs"—Critical and Creative thinking skills, Communication, and Collaboration—needed to become self-motivated lifelong learners, productive workers, and engaged citizens.

Learning how to manage learning projects more effectively gives students more time for exploring, learning, reflecting, and revising, and allows them to spend less time trying to keep their projects on track and dealing with team and process difficulties.

By combining PBL and project management in learning projects that reach beyond the school walls, students gain opportunities to engage in real-world, meaningful, and motivating activities that can make a real difference, no matter how small, in their own lives and their communities. Learning projects that involve internships, apprenticeships, service learning, or community volunteering often provide unforgettable experiences that can truly be life changing and career building.

Because more and more entry-level work in the job market involves project work and managing project responsibilities, learning effective project management practices early and throughout one's schooling years offers students a significant advantage in their transition into the work world. Given the very high level of youth unemployment in many

countries, work readiness is more crucial to a student's future success than ever before. Students with broad and deep experiences in managing learning projects throughout their school years will be much better equipped and ready to take on the jobs and challenges of our times.

What's in It for Educators?

We are currently preparing students
for jobs that don't yet exist,

using technologies that haven't been invented,

in order to solve problems we don't
even know are problems yet.

—Richard Riley, past U.S. Secretary of Education

As an educator and teacher, you know that preparing each and every student for success in a rapidly transforming world is one of the world's truly awesome challenges. The variety of expanding lists of "essential" competencies needed for success in a student's future—the knowledge, understandings, facts, data, basic skills, higher-order skills, character qualities, dispositions, mindsets, metacognitive strategies, plus all the core subjects of math, social studies, foreign language, science, coding, and so much more—can be totally overwhelming!

Teachers are increasingly discovering that there may be a simpler yet extremely powerful way to help prepare 21st century students for their futures, now that so many students have easier access to the world's facts and knowledge at their digital fingertips. There are three key strategies:

1. A focus on both *basic skills* (literacy, numeracy, and core social skills such as empathy) and a core set of *learning and doing skills* (such as the 4Cs—Critical and Creative thinking, Communication, and Collaboration)

2. Paying special attention to all students' motivations, interests, and *developing passions for learning something they really care about*, as a key to opening doors to deeper knowledge, building expertise and learning confidence, and then using this confidence to springboard to broader areas of learning

3. Using cross-subject collaborative learning projects as a way for students to develop a wider variety of applied knowledge and

skills, to interactively learn from one another and their teachers and advisors, and to practice their learning-and-doing skills through learning projects motivated by essential questions, problems, issues, or perspectives—the essence of effective PBL

These three learning strategies, combined with project management methods that support efficient and effective learning projects, can offer all students intensely motivating, engaging, and deeper learning experiences that increase their desire to learn more. These strategies also encourage further exploration of their interests and passions, increasing their capacity to quickly absorb wide areas of knowledge, producing results that often have real-world benefits. When the results of student projects are presented to an audience in a project fair or exhibition, other invaluable future-ready skills, such as persuasively communicating ideas to others, are also enhanced.

Students who learn the methods of project management and become effective project managers of their own learning can become helpful learning resources to others and be seen as student leaders. One expert project management–oriented high school teacher remarked:

> *Other teachers always tell me that they know instantly who my students are because they are the ones other students turn to for help when faced with managing a complex school project or event—they become the trusted leaders in their classes.*

What's in It for Parents?

I just want my child to be happy.
I want my son to be motivated, to stay in school.
I want the best for my child—to get into a good college.
I want my daughter to be ready to work in a good job.
I want her to be confident and successful,
prepared for her future.

—Parents on what they want for
their children's education

Happy, motivated, college-bound, work-ready, and prepped for success in learning, work, family and community life—these are some of the

qualities most parents say they want for their children and from their schools.

But what are we really readying our kids for—what kind of work, what kind of lifestyles, what sort of future? What do our children really need to learn now for a successful future?

First, as parents, we have to toss out our mental "rearview mirrors" of education past and look straight into our children's future. The future they will inhabit is a far cry from the world in which most parents grew up.

Just think of what more and more children have in their pockets and backpacks today:

- Mobile phones linking them to friends anywhere in the world with the tap of a social media icon;
- Vast global collections of information and media just a few clicks away;
- Instant answers to their factual questions with a short burst of phone thumb typing;
- Free access to gigantic libraries of "how-to" videos on virtually any topic and skill imaginable; and
- A portable studio for snapping, editing, and arranging photos, voice, and video recordings of their everyday life, instantly shared with friends and (sometimes) family.

It's light-years away from the paperbacks, comic books, pocket transistor radios, portable cassette players, and low- or no-tech toys from their parents' and grandparents' schooldays past. And given the pace of innovation in technical fields, it's even more light-years away from where technology will be just a couple of decades down the road.

Now think of today's jobs (and today's sometimes painful lack of them, especially for young people), and what work will be like when today's students graduate from their formal schooling, including:

- Large numbers of jobs moving to lower-wage countries;
- Low-wage service work on a steep rise;
- More highly demanding work involving complex thinking, communicating and creative innovating;
- High-tech tools used in practically every kind of job;
- Never-before-seen jobs in brand-new industries using just-invented technologies;

- Global corporations, global products, and global online marketing, sales, delivery and service;
- Rapidly rising global competition for high-paying jobs; and
- Growing importance of entrepreneurship—creating a job instead of finding one.

This is not even close to yesteryear's one-career-for-life position in a small business located nearby in town.

So how can parents best help their children get the learning experiences they need for a good life in the 21st century?

We have heard (and will hear much more in the rest of this book) about a core set of essential skills and mindsets that are keys to every student's successful future, and some particularly powerful ways to develop these capabilities. The project approach to learning presented in this book engages students in real-world challenges and provides motivated and structured opportunities to grow most of the competencies needed in the 21st century.

Parents everywhere can strongly support their child's developing readiness for the future by learning more about these simple project-oriented approaches and by encouraging their students to practice them at home and in their daily lives.

There are five things you can do as a parent to get started in helping your child be more future-ready:

1. Share your own expertise or passion for your work or hobby by taking a group of students to your workplace and showing them the kinds of projects you work on and what your work world is like, or by helping to organize and support a student project related to your work, skill, or hobby.
2. Encourage your child's teachers to do (and your principal and school board to support) more learning and service projects that focus on real-world issues.
3. Actively support your children's interests, hobbies, and passions (such as music, nature, art, inventing, etc.) and help children build both their knowledge and their skills while pursuing their passion through learning projects. Also let teachers know more about your children's strong interests and discuss how their personal passions can be incorporated into other schoolwork and learning experiences.

4. Try (and, admittedly, this is often a struggle) to steer your children's use of technology at home away from pure entertainment and social media use, and more toward online reading, researching, and creating things related to their interests (such as making a documentary video with friends, building an inventive physical device, creating a website on a famous person who shares their particular passion, etc.).

5. Use the resources in this book for helping your children and their friends better manage their learning projects and share these resources with teachers, schools, and other parents.

Moving our schools toward spending much more time on what our students need for their success is one of our century's great challenges.

And wouldn't all parents do whatever they can to have their child be successful . . . and happy, too?

Project Management as Learning, Work, and Life Skills

How Can Learning Projects Help All Students Become More Successful?

To see clearly how learning through projects can be so effective in motivating deeper learning experiences for both students and teachers, a real-world example of a highly successful project will be used throughout this chapter. The topic has universal appeal (and a touch of squeamish fascination), involving something that is literally vital to every one of our lives!

The Blood Project

The Blood Project combined art, science, medicine, and social studies, and also offered a social benefit to the community. This exemplary project comes from a high school in the High Tech High school network in San Diego, California (a brief video documentary of the project is available at http://youtu.be/LsJR2X-j7s4).

A science teacher and an art teacher combined efforts to have students research and create multimedia exhibits on some aspect of blood—from the history of the science of blood, to the role of blood in religion, to understanding AIDS, to the folklore of vampires, and much more.

Students created multimedia exhibits to be shown in a gallery next to a Red Cross blood bank to encourage people to donate blood (an example exhibit graphic is shown below).

The Blood Project will be used as an illustrative example throughout the following section, the Introductory Guide to Managing Learning Projects.

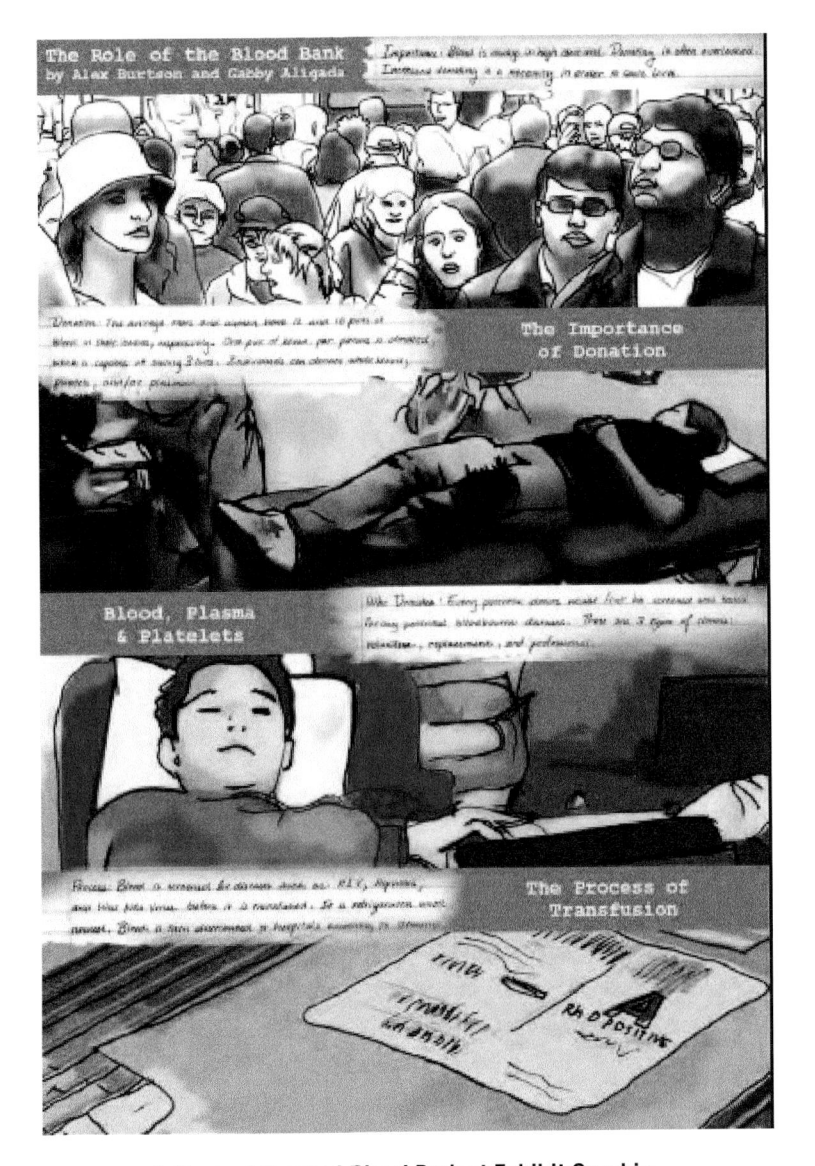

A Student-Created Blood Project Exhibit Graphic

Introductory Guide to Managing Learning Projects

(This section has been adapted from PMIEF's *Project Management for Learning—A Foundation Guide to Applying Project Management Principles and Methods to Education,* accessible at https://pmief.org/library/resources)

The world runs on projects—everyday life projects such as planning and planting a garden, school projects like devising and performing experiments for a science fair, and work-world projects like designing and building a bridge or developing and delivering a community program to reduce energy use.

The skills involved in managing and leading projects are essential *life skills*, *learning skills*, and *career skills,* as illustrated below:

Project Management and Leadership Pathways

Project Management and Leadership as a Set of *Life Skills*			
PreK–Primary	Middle	Secondary	Adult
Project Management and Leadership as a Set of *Learning Skills*			
PreK–Primary	Middle	Secondary	Adult
Project Management and Leadership as a Set of *Career Skills*			
PreK–Primary	Middle	Secondary	Adult

As a set of *life skills*, project methods can be learned starting at a very young age and continue throughout life (indicated by the yellow bar above).

As a progression of *learning skills*, students can begin applying project approaches to their education in the primary grades and continue through adulthood as lifelong learners (the green bar).

And as a series of developing *career skills*, students can begin learning the professional aspects of project management in later middle and secondary school and continue their learning throughout their careers, with some choosing project management as their profession (the blue bar).

In a very real sense, our own lives are far-reaching master projects, made of thousands of short- and long-term projects in living, learning, working, relating, and creating.

Much has been learned about how to (and how not to) effectively manage and lead projects—how each step in a project can be thoughtful, collaborative, productive, and creative, and how the learning gained in each project can empower students with the knowledge, skills, and personal qualities they need most for success throughout life.

For teachers, students, and parents, learning how to effectively manage and lead learning projects can be the key to developing more deeply engaged and self-motivated learners, more productive learning collaborations and project teamwork, more effective communications and compelling presentations, and a more creative and successful work life, an active community life, and a lifetime of enjoyable learning.

Project Cycle Terms Overview

Teachers and youth leaders who use learning projects in their classrooms and community centers know how incredibly motivating and engaging these projects can be for students. They also know how challenging projects can sometimes be—especially without clear guidance in how best to plan, organize, set up, launch, lead, manage, and make the most of all the moving parts in a rich learning project.

Applying the science and craft of project management to education requires some "translating" of professional terms and concepts into words, ideas, and images that are more readily accessible to educators and students. For this reason, in this guide, the professional terms used by the Project Management Institute (PMI) to describe the phases of a project are translated into more accessible, teacher- and student-friendly terms that fully align with the PMI professional project model as shown here:

Alignment of Educator-Friendly and Professional Project Cycle Terms

Life Skills Project Cycle Terms	Education-Learning Project Cycle Terms	Career-Professional Project Cycle Terms
Set a Goal	Define	Initiating
Plan the Steps	Plan	Planning
Do It	Do	Executing
		Monitoring/Controlling (also, throughout a project)
Review It	Review	Closing

In this guide, the learning project cycle terms are followed by the professional PMI terms in parentheses to show their alignment to the professional model—Define (Initiating), Plan (Planning), Do (Executing & Monitoring/Controlling), and Review (Closing). (See Project Learning for Educator Resources—Project Management Pathways on pages 88–89 for more details.)

Projects offer students rich opportunities to learn how to manage and lead effective projects, hone a variety of essential 21st century skills (especially the 4Cs—Critical and Creative thinking, Communicating, and Collaborating), and apply these skills to deepen their knowledge of the world, themselves, and others, and to help build a better world through impactful projects.

Projects Defined

Each of us is involved in all sorts of projects throughout our lives, but unless you're a project management professional, we don't often think about what makes a project a project.

All around us are things to be done, tasks to accomplish, decisions to be made, skills to learn, problems to solve, and results to achieve. For example:

- Families decide what to buy at the food market, purchase the items, and make meals;
- Farmers plant, cultivate, and harvest crops that are then sold in markets;
- New houses are planned, designed, constructed, and sold, and families move into them;
- Teachers plan their lessons, engage students in activities, and evaluate the results;
- Students receive assignments, do research, and write up and present their findings;
- Communities develop recycling plans, implement them, and measure the impact; and
- Businesses plan new products, develop and test them, and sell them to consumers.

What makes all of these diverse activities, from small to large, projects? They all have two key qualities:

1. Projects are *temporary* efforts with a clear start and finish—they are not ongoing, and
2. Projects have an *end result*—something created or completed that is often unique.

In the examples above, some of the end project results include eating meals, food sold in grocery stores, families moving into new homes, school lessons learned, research papers handed in, recycling impact reports presented, and new products sold in stores and online.

Listening to the daily weather and stock market reports, answering your phone, brushing your teeth each night—these kinds of activities are not usually considered projects because they are brief, ongoing activities, and though there are some short-term results, there isn't much of an end result in mind. These simple actions just keep recurring regularly and they don't really require an intentional plan or produce a result that's complex, different, new, or unique.

Everyday Life Projects

Let's take the example above of a simple, everyday project—deciding what to buy at the grocery store, then going out and buying the items. What are the possible steps involved?

1. Announce that you're going shopping for food.
2. Ask what family members would like from the food market and make a shopping list.
3. Travel to the market and buy what's on the list, then bring the items home.
4. Make sure everything on the list was purchased.

Though this seems like a very simple activity that doesn't need a great deal of thought or effort to accomplish, the four steps involved in going food shopping highlight the common steps in everyday projects:

1. *Set a goal*—buy some food for meals.
2. *Plan the steps*—make a list.

3. *Do it*—go shopping.
4. *Review it*—check if you got everything on the list.

Because this is a recurring project (and not just an ongoing activity that doesn't need a plan), you can consider these steps to be a repeating cycle of project work, producing unique results each time the four project phases are completed, as shown here:

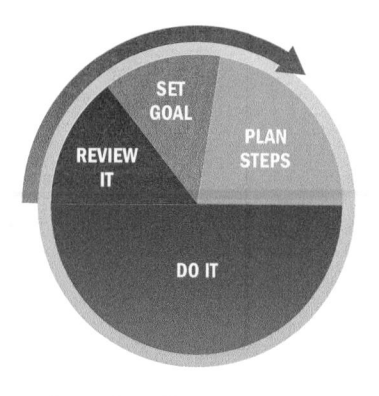

Everyday Life Project Cycle

Even with this simple, short-term project example, you can see where there might be a number of opportunities to improve the process and results of the project, such as in the following ways:

- In *setting a goal*—you might consider if there are enough items needed to justify a trip to the food market or if there's enough food already in your kitchen or available from your garden that would make shopping less necessary, etc.
- In *planning the steps*—checking to see what is already in the pantry or refrigerator, discussing what is affordable, seeing if there are special deals or coupons that could be used to lower the cost of the food, determining if this project could be combined with other errands to be more efficient, deciding which method of transportation should be used, etc.
- In *doing it*—dividing up the list among family members so that the shopping goes faster, making sure to choose the best quality for price for each item on your shopping list, adding

items to your list to take advantage of unexpected special deals in the store, making on-the-spot decisions not to purchase items because of poor quality or high price, etc.

- In *reviewing it*—evaluating if the ingredients purchased are healthy and taste good in the meals, checking if friends know of better deals in other markets, deciding not to purchase certain items again or to search for better items in other markets, starting an updated shopping list for the next shopping trip, etc.

For simple projects like shopping for food, we don't usually need to spend a lot of time planning and trying our best to make sure the goal is clear, that all the steps are thoroughly planned for maximum efficiency, that teamwork is well coordinated and productive, or that the best quality for the lowest cost is achieved—we just go food shopping and improvise as best as we can, and things generally turn out well enough.

But think of a highly complex, large-scale project, with thousands of intricate technical tasks, hundreds of team members, and very little room for the slightest error—such as landing a mobile robotic science lab on the surface of Mars—and you can see why the profession of project management has become so important to almost every field of study and work in today's complex and interconnected world.

Learning Projects and 21ˢᵗ Century Skills

The list of what students need for success in today's world is expanding, and the knowledge, skills, and personal qualities needed to do well in school, work, family, and civic life stretch well beyond basic literacy, numeracy, and facts in a few core subject areas. New learning methods are needed to help master this broader set of essential skills and competencies.

The movement to widen the goals of learning for success has been called a variety of names by a number of educational organizations and leaders, including *21ˢᵗ Century Skills, Deeper Learning, College and Career Readiness, Next Generation Learning, Student Centered Learning,* and others. Regardless of the name, there is a growing global consensus that skills such as the ones listed below (from the Partnership for 21ˢᵗ Century Learning) are essential for success in our times.

21ˢᵗ Century Skills from the Partnership for 21ˢᵗ Century Learning

Learning and Innovation Skills "The 4Cs"	Digital Literacy Skills	Career and Life Skills
Critical thinking and problem solving	Information literacy	Flexibility and adaptability
Creativity and innovation	Media literacy	Initiative and self-direction
Communication	ICT (information and communications technology) literacy	Social and cross-cultural fluency
Collaboration	Productivity and accountability	Leadership and responsibility

(See Project Learning Resources–21ˢᵗ Century Skills Descriptions on pages 90–97, and for more information about the Partnership for 21ˢᵗ Century Learning go to: http://www.p21.org)

To acquire and reach high levels of proficiency in these skills, students need sequences of learning experiences that give them lots of opportunities to practice and improve each of these skills.

Learning projects, or project based learning (PBL), as they are commonly called, are a powerful approach to learning offering a wealth of opportunities to build all of these essential 21ˢᵗ century skills, as well as the deeper knowledge and expertise needed for work and life in our times.

Learning Project Phases

Similar to the project steps in the food shopping project outlined above, learning projects have four phases that occur in a sequence, though backtracking and jumping around among the phases is common.

The four learning project phases (and their corresponding PMI terms) are:

1. Define (Initiating),
2. Plan (Planning),
3. Do (Executing & Monitoring/Controlling), and
4. Review (Closing).

A learning project must first be *defined*, with the question, problem, issue, or perspective that drives the learning in the project stated clearly and concisely.

In the Blood Project described above, the defining challenge for this project was the question: "How might we combine art and science in an exhibit that visually explains some aspect of blood that will engage

community members and encourage them to give blood to a blood bank?"

Both the art and science teachers had a lot of collaborative *planning* to do for this project—preparing lessons on the science of blood, developing skill-building activities in designing and creating compelling multimedia exhibits, planning and supporting student research on their particular topic and on what convinces people to donate their blood to a blood bank, and a whole lot more.

For teachers to be effective learning coaches for their students during a project, they need to provide opportunities for students to learn skills such as problem solving, collaboration, textual and visual communication, and creative design (lectures alone will not lead to project success here!).

Learning activities must also be designed so that students own much of their own planning and work. Choosing their topic to research and serve as the focus of their exhibit, deciding who should be part of the project team and what their roles should be, taking on leadership and support roles in the teamwork, managing the research, sharing their findings with others, and incorporating feedback are all important parts of a good learning project that hones skills and deepens understanding.

After planning comes the *doing*: The real work of the project must be done—the research, design, and creation of the exhibit must be completed and set up for display. Teachers and students work together, with the teachers playing the "conductor" or coach role, and the students taking on the role of "researchers, designers, and creators" as team members in the project.

Finally, the project results and lessons learned are presented and *reviewed*—in the Blood Project, by the public as well as other students, teachers, and family members. The individual and group learning gained in the project, and the impact the team project has on the community (hopefully an increase in the number of blood donations), are evaluated, and further feedback, praise, suggestions for improvements, and recognition of project accomplishments are all shared.

Project Learning Cycle Overview

Define, Plan, Do, and *Review (Initiating, Planning, Executing & Monitoring/Controlling,* and *Closing)* are the phases in the project learning and

teaching cycles—the project "wheels" for both teachers and students as illustrated here:

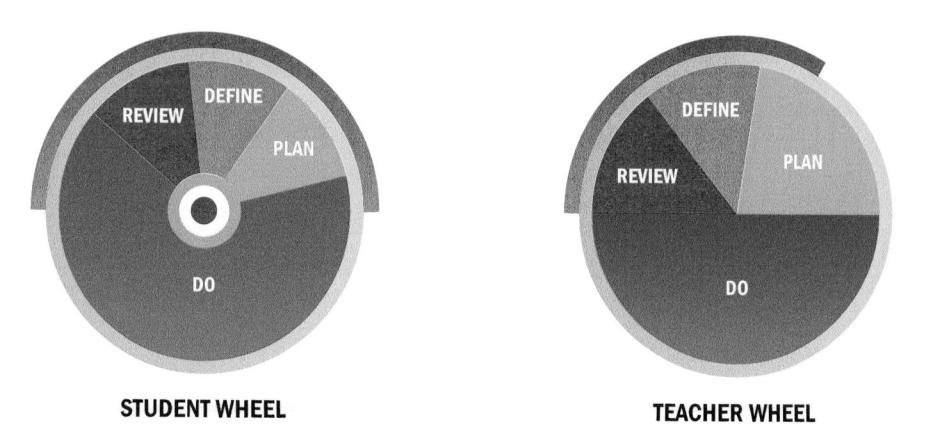

STUDENT WHEEL   **TEACHER WHEEL**

Project Cycle Wheels for Students and Teachers

Though time spent in each of the phases of a learning project may differ for teachers and students—teachers typically spend more time in up-front planning and students spend more time in the doing phase of project activities (hence, the different sizes of the wheel segments above)—both teachers and students work together to co-manage the entire project as shown here:

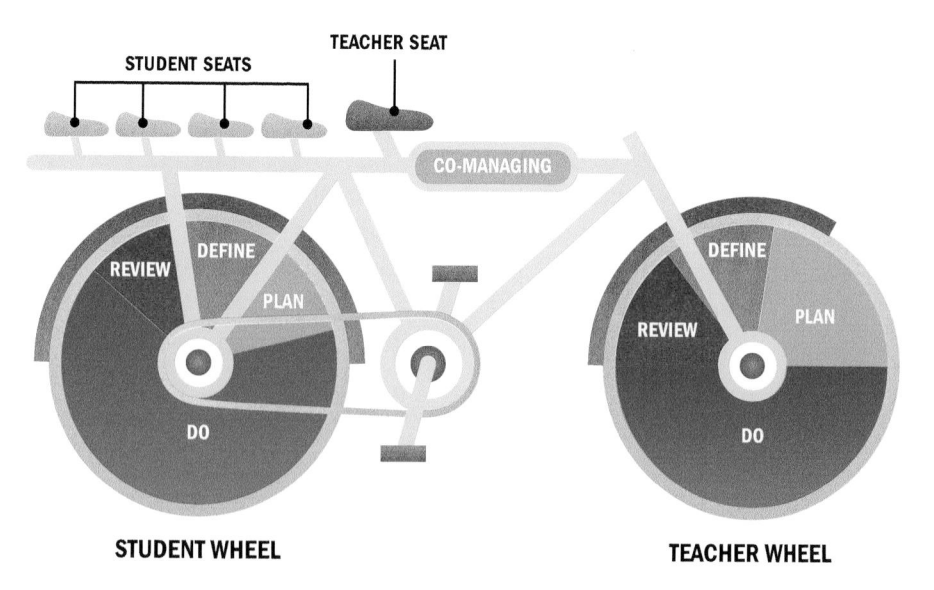

STUDENT WHEEL   **TEACHER WHEEL**

The Project Cycle Frame and Wheels

With the project's wheels and framework in place, we need the other essential components to complete our two-wheeled project learning vehicle: the handlebars, gears, brakes, and cyclometer to measure progress as shown here:

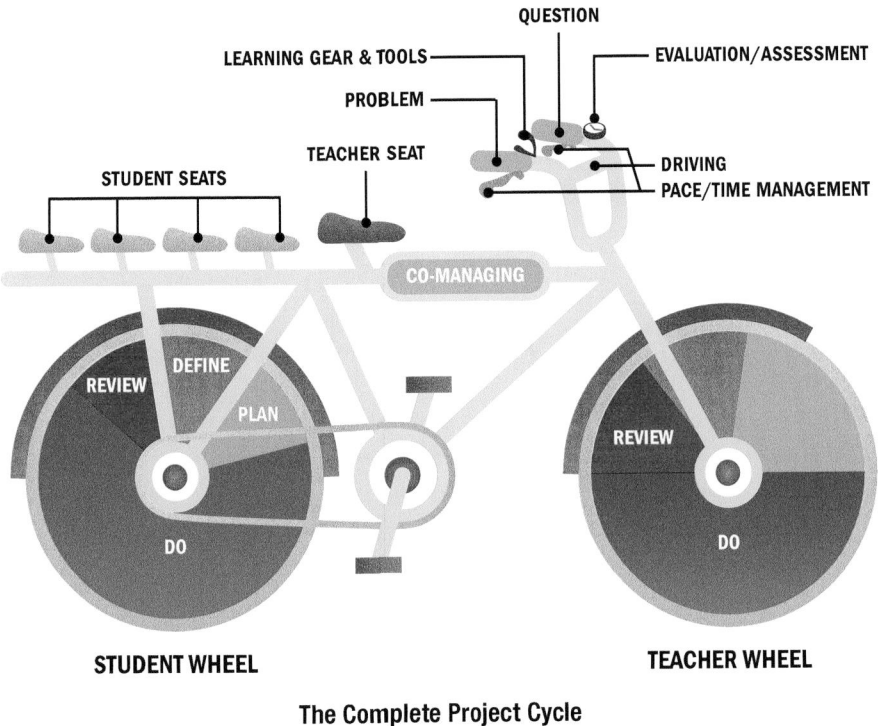

The Complete Project Cycle

The handlebars represent the project's driving challenge—the question, problem, issue, or perspective that sets the direction and motivation for the project and keeps it on course.

The learning gear used in the project (books, laptops, internet access, design software, etc.) is signified by the gearshift lever—projects with more powerful learning tools and the ability to use them well are "geared up" for more powerful learning.

The pace and timing of a project—not too fast, not too slow, adjusted for the learning needs of team members—is indicated by the handbrakes and the pedals.

The cyclometer represents the ongoing evaluations of student work—giving real-time feedback so adjustments can be made as the project

progresses—which are essential for correcting misunderstandings and improving the outcomes in each phase of the learning project.

Once the project is launched and "on the road," the slope of the road-way denotes the degree of challenge that the project presents to the team—steep uphill climbs with complex, demanding projects being more challenging than flat-surface, simple, straightforward projects.

Balance is important, too. For example, if the project cycle leans too far to the right, the teacher may be oversteering and applying too much direct instructional control for the students to exercise their self-direction and ownership of the project; too far to the left, and there may be too much independent and uncoordinated work going in too many directions (otherwise known as chaos) preventing deeper learning from happening.

Support from school administrators, parents, and community members can provide a nice tail wind to help propel a project; lack of such support could result in strong headwinds to thwart the project's progress.

And last, but certainly not least, the destination road sign, as shown below, indicates the larger goal of every well-designed project: a rich learning experience that blends knowledge, understanding, and deep personal engagement in building the skills and expertise needed for success in 21st century learning, work, and life:

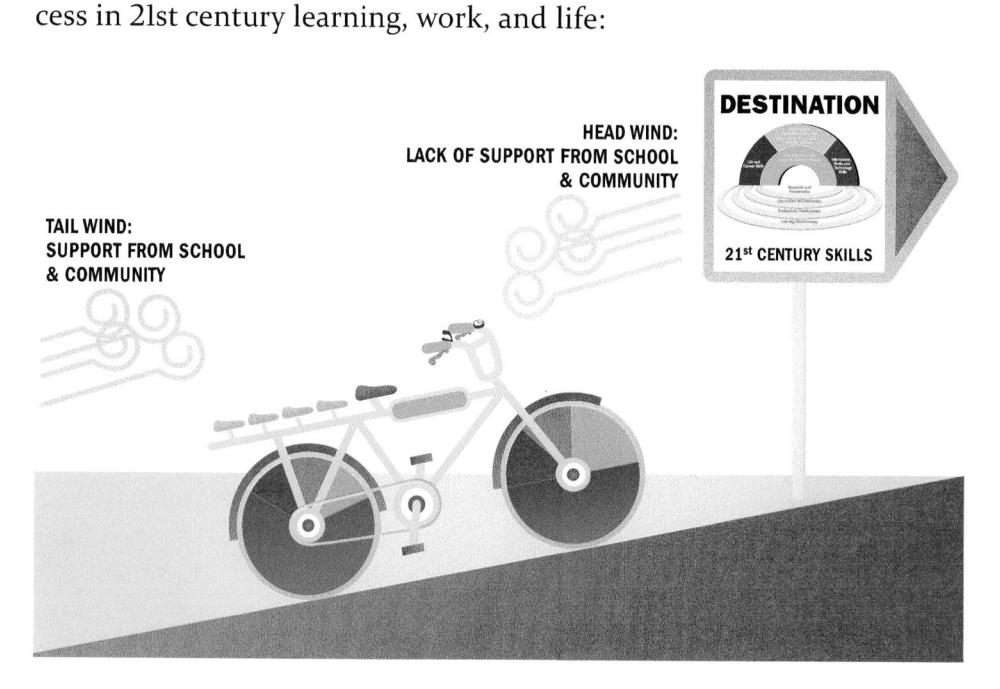

The Project Cycle on the Project Road

Designing, managing, and leading compelling 21ˢᵗ century learning projects, like the Blood Project, is no small challenge. It has to engage and motivate a wide diversity of students, meet the curriculum goals of the school, align to learning standards, provide evidence that each student is gaining understanding and proficiency, and prepare students for success in the real world.

Understanding how projects work and how to effectively support, manage, and lead a wide variety of learning projects enables teachers and students to focus more on each student's learning goals and get the most out of each and every project for each and every learner.

Types of Learning Projects—Inquiry and Design

Though there may seem to be infinite types of learning projects across all fields of knowledge and possible areas of student and teacher interests—from art to zoology—for the purposes of managing and leading learning projects, it is useful to identify four common learning project types, with many projects having a mix of two or more of these project types or "flavors" as shown in the table below:

Common Types of Learning Projects

Project Types	Learning Motivation	End Result
INQUIRY	Question	Answer
DESIGN	Problem	Solution
DEBATE	Issue	Position
EXPRESSION	Perspective	Performance

Inquiry projects start with a *question*: Why is the sky blue? What causes cancer? How does burning fossil fuels affect the climate?

Questions naturally fuel the desire to find answers, through research, asking experts, doing experiments to test possible answers, and by comparing answers with others who are researching the same questions.

The learning power of the right question at the right time has been celebrated throughout history. Philosophers, education theorists, and thought leaders have placed questioning and inquiry—the search for the truth—at the heart of learning and understanding.

One legendary example is Einstein's early question about what it would be like to travel on a light beam, which initiated a lifelong quest

to understand the universe that led to some of the greatest discoveries in 20th century physics.

In contrast, design projects start with a *problem*: How can we make airplane travel safer? How can we store more information in a smaller space? How can we use the sun's energy to heat and power our homes?

Problems demand solutions, and the motivation to create solutions to problems leads to researching and comparing how others have solved similar problems, designing, building, testing, and refining possible solutions, and sometimes coming up with innovative solutions that change the course of history.

One memorable example of the hunt for solutions is Thomas Edison's well-known year-and-a-half-long search for the right materials to make an effective incandescent electric light bulb, which eventually resulted in lighting up the world for people everywhere.

Questions and problems and inquiry and design projects are the foundations for two of the most powerful approaches humankind has yet developed for discovering new knowledge and creating new ways of living: science and engineering.

Though the project methods are similar in inquiry and design projects and in science and engineering, there are some differences in the way answers and solutions are devised and tested as shown here:

Inquiry/Scientific and Design/Engineering Project Phases

Project Phases	Inquiry Project Methods (including the Scientific Method)	Design Project Methods (including Engineering Design methods)
Define (Initiating)	Pose a question	Define a problem
Plan (Planning)	Research the question	Research the problem
	Formulate an answer, explanation, or hypothesis that can be tested	Design and plan a prototype or solution to be tested
Do (Executing & Monitoring/ Controlling)	Test the hypothesis through experiments or other methods that attempt to disprove it	Create and test the prototype or solution to see if it solves the problem
Review (Closing)	Analyze the results and draw a conclusion about the answer	Analyze the results and improve the solution to the problem
	Communicate and present the results and compare with others' results	Communicate and demonstrate the results and decide to implement or market the solution as a product or service
Next Cycle	Repeat the process with more refined questions or with new questions that arose in the inquiry process	Repeat the process with refined or new ideas for better solutions, or with new problems that arose in the design process

Types of Learning Projects—Debate and Expression

Making a compelling case backed by strong evidence—for a change in policy, a legal decision, a new regulation or law, a business plan or investment, a contribution to a philanthropic cause, a decision to vote for a candidate or to take one course of action over another, and so on—is the lifeblood of civic and community life, the heart of governing and lawmaking at all levels, the core of making good business decisions, and the collaborative give-and-take process by which societies evolve to meet new demands.

Projects centered on a debate over a set of complex or controversial issues help students:

- Exercise their critical listening and thinking skills;
- Hone their note-taking, writing, speaking, and persuasion skills;
- Work productively in teams to research facts and collaboratively develop convincing arguments;
- Advance their information and media literacy skills;
- Identify common flaws in logic and techniques that may distort the truth;
- Strengthen their rational argumentation, refutation, and reasoning skills; and
- Build confidence in public speaking and thinking on their feet in answering questions and arguing for a position on the issue.

Whether the project results in a formal debate or a series of presentations arguing for a specific position on an issue, debate-oriented projects build the skills necessary for a lifetime of thoughtful engagement in civic, political, social, and community life.

In contrast, projects based on the artful expressions of students' perspectives, thoughts, feelings, desires, ambitions, and dreams, giving voice to the full range of their experiences and emotions through music, art, dance, theater, poetry, crafts, or a media mix of these expressive forms, is especially important to students' healthy psychological and social development.

All too often, so much emphasis is placed on academic performance and externally directed extracurricular activities that time to engage students' personal reflections and to give voice to deeper thoughts and feelings is very limited.

There is increasing evidence that students who are given the time to reflect and self-direct more of their learning, who are offered opportunities to produce meaningful artifacts and expressions of their self-image and their relationships to others, and are regularly shown evidence of their positive growth and learning, will develop more positive mindsets and beliefs about themselves, their meaning and purpose, their ability to overcome barriers, their confidence to tackle and persist through tough challenges, and their ability to develop a variety of positive relationships with others.

Collective forms of expression, as in music, dance, and theater performances, and in the collaborative creation of audio, video, and multimedia compositions, also build social and teamwork skills, empathy and negotiation abilities, and strategies for helping and supporting others that are valuable for learning, work, and community life.

Debate and expression-oriented learning projects have differing goals and methods, but both types of projects help build personal, expressive, and social skills essential for future success, as outlined here:

Debate and Personal Expression Project Phases

Project Phases	Issue Debate Project Methods	Personal Expression Project Methods
Define (Initiating)	Choose an issue	Reflect on a personal perspective, idea, feeling, ambition, dream, vision, etc.
Plan (Planning)	Research the issue	Choose a medium of expression (words, music, video, dance, art, etc.)
	Form a position, based on strong evidence, verified facts, well-founded opinions of experts, etc.	Design, plan and create an outline, storyboard, sketch, prototype, etc., of the perspective, message, and feelings you hope to communicate to others
Do (Executing & Monitoring/ Controlling)	Present the position and evidence and logically argue its strengths and possible drawbacks, rationally refute opposition to the position, etc.	Test the prototype, rough draft, demo, or outline of the work on others to see if it communicates your intention, then create and perform or display the work for an audience
Review (Closing)	Assess the impact of the presentation of the case on others—through polling, surveying, voting, observed actions taken, policies changed, etc.	Evaluate your own views and feelings about the performance of the work—did it express what you wanted it to?—then gauge the reaction from the audience by discussing the messages and feelings they had from experiencing the work
	Capture the results of your efforts to present and defend your position in your portfolio of student work	Reflect on the entire expression project and record your thoughts and feelings along with a recording of the performance or display of the work for your portfolio
Next Cycle	Repeat the process with better research and stronger arguments to strengthen the case for your position, or your new position on the issue, or develop a new position for a new issue related to the previous one, in the next debate or presentation	Repeat the process by further developing and improving the original work or developing a new expression that arose out of the creative process in the original work

Being aware of the differing goals and methods of project types can help teachers and students design the appropriate project experiences that help achieve the learning goals that are important to each learner. Often, a mix of a couple of project types as subprojects in one master project can offer students a wider variety of experiences that appeal to different personal interests and can develop a wider array of skills, understandings, and mindsets, all within one learning project.

Project Based Learning (PBL) and Project Management (PM)

How Do PBL and PM Work Together?

Brief History of Project Based Learning (PBL)

The idea of using applied projects for learning is not new. Architects, painters, and sculptors in 16th century Italy desired to be thought of as much more than skilled artisans like stone masons and carpenters, who learned their craft through oral tradition and apprenticeship practices. They wanted to be considered professionals with special training that combined deep scientific knowledge with a wide variety of applied creative skills.

To achieve this status, they needed a professional school that would combine science, art, and craft into one curricular program. In 1577, under the patronage of Pope Gregory XIII, the Accademia di San Luca was founded in Rome.

It was here that traditional lectures were combined with the construction of imaginative and creative scale models of buildings, churches, monuments, and palaces. These applied projects were called *progetti* (projects). Twenty years later, these *progetti* evolved into project competitions in which student projects were officially evaluated by a standard set of criteria (today we call them educational "rubrics").

That was the beginning (or at least the earliest documentation) of project based learning in education.

Even these early learning projects had many characteristics of what today would be called "Gold Standard PBL." The projects involved the following:

- *Challenges*—a question, problem, issue, or perspective that needed deep knowledge, skills, and mindsets to tackle successfully
- *Authentic*, real-world experiences, with real deadlines and a demand for quality results, with the results reviewed by real working professionals, not short, made-up academic exercises or artificial problem sets
- Student *voice* and *choice,* with multiple "right" answers and the opportunities to present one's thinking and skills through creative work
- *Public products* that students present for feedback and review—an example of making the learning visible to others
- *Critiques and revisions,* where students receive ongoing valuable feedback from peers and professionals alike, authentically motivating their further learning and skill building

The development of PBL in education to the present has been a long journey with many twists and turns, involving such notable educators and theorists as William Kilpatrick, John Dewey, Maria Montessori, Jean Piaget, Seymour Papert, and many others.

In 2015 (438 years after the founding of the Accademia di San Luca), the Buck Institute for Education researched and summarized the essential elements of high-quality PBL design and practice, based on over 20 years of experience in promoting, developing, and training teachers and educators in PBL. The results are captured in two Gold Standard PBL diagrams shown on the next page.

Brief History of Project Management

Though there is a great deal of speculation, little is known for sure about the earliest project management methods used to build the Great Pyramid of Giza or the Great Wall of China because the management methods used were not well recorded.

It wasn't until 1917 that the first officially published project management process was created by Henry Gantt—the scheduling diagram

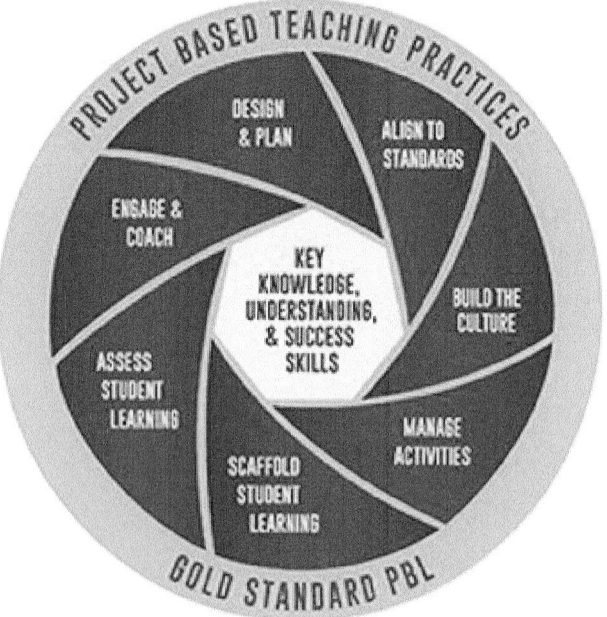

Buck Institute for Education's Gold Standard PBL Diagrams

with his name on it, still in use today: the *Gantt Chart*. Gantt is considered the founding father of modern project management. One of the first uses of his *Gantt Chart* was on the U.S. Hoover Dam project of 1931.

A slew of project management tools, methods, and organizations appeared in the 1950s and 1960s, including the following:

- The American Association of Cost Engineers (now AACE International) was formed in 1956.
- The *Critical Path Method (CPM)* was invented by the DuPont Corporation in 1957.
- The *Program Evaluation Review Technique (PERT)* was invented for the U.S. Navy's Polaris Project to manage time and tasks in a large missile project in 1958.
- The U.S. Defense Department created the *Work Breakdown Structure (WBS)* approach to better manage tasks in 1962.
- The International Project Management Association (IPMA) was founded in 1965.
- The Project Management Institute (PMI) was launched by five volunteers (including Jim Snyder, the author of this book's foreword) in Pennsylvania to promote the project management profession in 1969.

From then on, project management tools, methodologies, and organizations have multiplied and expanded, and the number of professional project managers has mushroomed, making project management one of the fastest-growing professions, and PMI one of the fastest-growing professional associations, in the world.

In 1990, PMI founded a nonprofit public charitable organization, the Project Management Institute Educational Foundation (PMIEF), to bring the power of project management principles and practices to the rest of society beyond business, especially in education, disaster recovery, and improving the project effectiveness of nonprofit organizations.

PMIEF's education work over the years has resulted in a wide variety of resources to help teachers, students, parents, and education administrators apply PM principles and practices to their learning, their work, and their lives. (See the PMIEF website for the latest list of *Learning Resources for Educators* at https://pmief.org/library/resources)

PM + PBL = Future-Ready Students, Schools, and Societies

We now know that preparing students for a project based world is essential. Projects have become a central unit of work in the workforce and the main organizing method in civic, social, and political change initiatives. PBL is rapidly becoming a widespread instructional method in schools and educational programs worldwide.

Managing one's learning, work, and civic and community participation through projects has become an essential set of lifelong and life-wide skills.

The power of learning projects to help transform how schools teach and how students learn what's needed for future success has been well documented. (See the Project Learning Resources—Educational Research on Project Learning section of this book on pages 99–103 for a research summary of the benefits of project learning approaches.)

By integrating the deep work, expertise, and developments of both PBL educator networks and PM professional communities of practice, many exciting innovations and transformations are already occurring, with much more to come. These include the following:

- PMIEF is working with the Buck Institute for Education to identify best practices in project learning design, practice, and management. The findings will be the basis for a series of educator guides to world-class, exemplary PBL and project management learning practices.
- PMIEF is supporting a Project Learning Network of educational organization leaders who actively promote the use of learning projects in education. This network is actively sharing best practices, and PMIEF is supporting a number of initiatives to build more effective strategies and practices to deepen the learning value of PBL and project management in education, and to widen and scale up the effective use of educational learning projects across the globe.
- Several international project based student competitions are adopting project management materials for their competition guides, including Destination Imagination, the Model UN program, Future Cities, FIRST Robotics, and others.
- The George Lucas Educational Foundation is developing a series of Advanced Placement courses for secondary schools

that are highly project oriented, based on a thorough review of the research on project learning design and management.

- Digital Promise is now hosting project management for educator micro-credentials on its online platform. These micro-credentials provide digital badges for teachers who successfully submit the work outlined in each micro-credential and have their work judged to be of high quality by expert educators. The micro-credential submissions include two examples of student work, teacher explanations of the activities and evaluations they used with their students, and both teacher and student reflections on what was learned.

- As the need for skilled workers in the STEM fields (science, technology, engineering, and mathematics, or alternatively, the DREAMS fields—design, research, engineering, arts, mathematics and science) rapidly increases, the importance of a project approach to these fields is clear. Examples of initiatives in these areas include DiscoverE's integrated Project Management/Engineering Design process for their Future Cities competition, mapping the project cycle phases to the engineering design phases, as shown in the graphic on the next page, from their competition guide.

In short, the prospects have never been better for PBL and project management coming together in ever more powerful ways to propel learning progress through well-designed and well-managed learning projects.

More and more project-oriented educators and leaders are sharing their successes and challenges in helping all students gain the skills needed for future success. Opportunities for even more widespread adoption of PBL and project management approaches are rapidly growing, ensuring that more students, schools, and eventually, whole societies, will be well on their way to becoming project-savvy and future-ready, capable of designing, managing, and implementing highly impactful projects that tackle the complex challenges of our time.

CREATE YOUR FUTURE CITY!

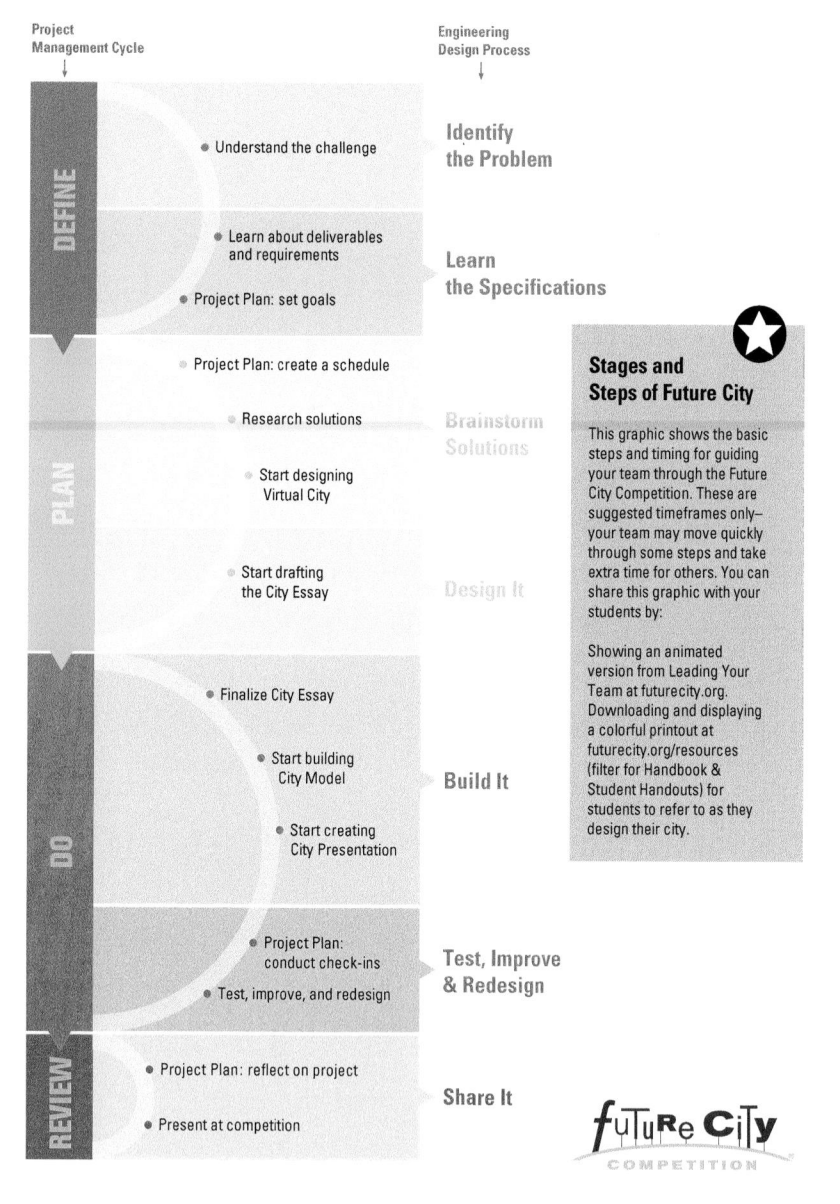

Project Management Cycle

Engineering Design Process

DEFINE
- Understand the challenge
- Learn about deliverables and requirements
- Project Plan: set goals

Identify the Problem

Learn the Specifications

PLAN
- Project Plan: create a schedule
- Research solutions
- Start designing Virtual City
- Start drafting the City Essay

Brainstorm Solutions

Design It

DO
- Finalize City Essay
- Start building City Model
- Start creating City Presentation

Build It

REVIEW
- Project Plan: conduct check-ins
- Test, improve, and redesign
- Project Plan: reflect on project
- Present at competition

Test, Improve & Redesign

Share It

Stages and Steps of Future City

This graphic shows the basic steps and timing for guiding your team through the Future City Competition. These are suggested timeframes only—your team may move quickly through some steps and take extra time for others. You can share this graphic with your students by:

Showing an animated version from Leading Your Team at futurecity.org. Downloading and displaying a colorful printout at futurecity.org/resources (filter for Handbook & Student Handouts) for students to refer to as they design their city.

Future Cities Competition Project Management/Engineering Design Integration

*Time is at once the most valuable and the
most perishable of all our possessions.*

—John Randolph

The Timeless Time Management Challenge

How Can We Help Students Tackle This Lifelong Motivational Challenge?

Time and the Speed of Thinking

Despite mountains of self-help and management books, articles, and countless tips on how to understand and manage time, there still remains a great deal of confusion on how best to think about and effectively use our precious time, especially the time devoted to working on large projects.

Even with an amazing variety of available scheduling, task, time, and project work management tools and techniques, time management continues to present a difficult challenge, especially for students.

In a groundbreaking book called, *Thinking, Fast and Slow,* Daniel Kahneman offered a well-researched, two-part systems model of how our everyday thinking works, and how this relates to the way we spend our time, or more often, avoid spending it.

In Kahneman's model, System 1 is our fast, automatic, intuitive, emotional, and somewhat unconscious thinking mode—how we immediately complete phrases such as "One and one is . . ." and how we quickly respond to the emotional tone of someone's speech. System 1 has come in very handy during our human evolution, when instant responses to the cracking sound of a tree branch could mean either life or death.

System 2, on the other hand, is our slow, intentional, rational, analytical, and consciously effortful mode of reasoning about the world and the work ahead. It is how we approach doing long division, filling out our taxes, designing and building a house, and writing a book.

System 2 has one very significant additional feature: It is lazy and tires easily. Too often, instead of slowing down and rationally analyzing a situation, making careful plans, and methodically breaking down all the work that needs to be done, System 2 is content to accept the more expedient System 1 responses and avoid all that energy-expending brainwork.

Given this strong System 2 tendency to save thinking energy by avoiding tedious mental effort, we can see why procrastination is so widespread and why we invent so many clever ways to avoid long and complex mental challenges. We can also see why we often choose to get thinking tasks over with as quickly as possible with the least amount of work, and why we like to pick the first or easiest solution that comes to mind.

Avoiding lots of complex and deep thinking is actually *wired into the way our brains work*!

So, how do we overcome this inherent avoidance of slow thinking and use our time productively to get challenging and detailed project work done?

Time Management = Motivation + Flow Management

> *In truth, people can generally make time*
> *for what they choose to do; it is not really*
> *the time but the will that is lacking.*
> **—Sir John Lubbock**

Both PBL-oriented teachers and project managers know that when everyone on a project team is motivated by the goals or mission of a project, if team members believe that the work they are doing is really meaningful, and if everyone has chosen to do her/his part to make the team and the overall project successful, the time management challenge becomes less of a hurdle. In fact, when all these conditions are in place, it's often hard to stop students from continuing their work on their projects!

Here's how one student (who worked on the Blood Project described in Educator Chapter 2) talked about the motivational and learning impact a project can have:

> *We learned about the astounding life that blood*
> *brings to society. It travels through our heart,*
> *oxygenates our brains and bodies, protects us from*
> *diseases, simply keeping us alive. At the same time,*
> *we had the opportunity to share its message with*
> *our community. Without it we cannot strive, live, or*
> *even have the opportunity to give. When there are*
> *flaws, we have epidemics such as AIDS, or leukemia,*
> *or anemia. At the same time, blood is prevalent in*
> *entertainment. Without so much as a drop in action*
> *or horror movies, there would be no Hollywood.*
>
> *This opportunity was nothing like I have ever had,*
> *and looking back, it was the most work, but the*
> *most fulfilling project I've done in high school.*
>
> **—Gabby Aligada, 12th grade**

What this student is describing in her exciting project work can be seen as a highly motivated state of *flow*, the term used by psychology researcher Mihaly Csikszentmihalyi in his book *Flow: The Psychology of Optimal Experience.* Flow may be the most important antidote we have for overcoming our inborn reluctance to do slow, hard thinking.

When one is in the flow state, concentration, deep thinking, problem solving, and complex analysis becomes much easier and more natural. What's more, *time seems to slow down and stress about time and deadlines turns into fulfilling and enjoyable experiences that students want to go on and on.*

There are a number of conditions that help students and project team members achieve a state of flow in their learning projects, based on a large body of research into the phenomenon. Here are nine of them:

1. Project goals are clear, meaningful, relevant, and exciting to everyone.
2. Project challenges are attainable—not too hard, not too easy.
3. Students can choose the challenges they take on—they have project ownership.

4. Students have an environment that supports deep concentration when needed.
5. There is enough time for focused work to continue without interruptions.
6. Students have an environment that supports a variety of hands-on experiences.
7. Students get clear and quick feedback as they progress so they can adjust their work.
8. Students have positive relations with their team, teacher, project manager, etc.
9. Laughter and celebrations of good work are always welcome.

Effective teachers and project managers have learned how to create project environments and practices that support these conditions, making the flow state happen more often for more students and project teams.

In short, our timeless time management challenges are really motivational challenges that can be overcome by a strong internal drive and commitment to a project's goals and a project culture and environment that encourages flow experiences to happen.

Though scheduling, *Work Breakdown Structures*, *Gantt Charts*, and other project management tools are still extremely helpful in tracking and managing project work, nurturing personal motivation and flow experiences may be the most powerful methods we have to ensure that deep learning, high-quality results, productive team processes, and, of course, project deadlines, are all achieved in well-managed, engaging learning projects.

Agile and Adaptive Learning Project Methods

How Can Adaptive Methods Build Engagement, Discovery, and Motivation?

Who and What "Drives" the Learning Project?

Projects can originate (and transform) in many ways: Teachers can engage students in a project of their own design, students can start with an idea and develop it into a full project, or frequently, there is a discovery stage where both students and teachers explore possible project ideas and then collaborate on project designs that capture students' interests and motivations and also cover the needed areas of the curriculum.

At Matthew Moss High School in Greater Manchester (United Kingdom), students have taken on projects including building a catapult, designing and making T-shirts "from scratch," building a car engine from parts, and refereeing a netball match (this challenge was chosen by a student whose great love of netball helped to overcome some of his severe learning difficulties).

Teacher Mark Moorhouse gives an entertaining account of how the Car Engine project developed from students' general interest in fast cars to a serious and deep learning undertaking:

> *A group of three students wanted to do a project on cars. In this instance, the "scrutiny phase," in which their learning*

plan is challenged by both me and the rest of the class, was paramount. I suggested that the learning from taking a high-performance engine apart would be real and significant and they'd actually get to find things out and push themselves. They were really excited by the reality of it—real engine, real tools—and off we went.

As luck would have it, I had three expired Subaru EJ20TT engines at a friend's garage. Initially I planned to bring a complete unit in for the students to strip, but I started to worry about the toxicity of old engine oil and health and safety. Then I remembered that my friend and I had one already stripped and cleaned in bits. So the challenge evolved to building the engine from bits—just as good and far cleaner and safer.

While the students were searching on the internet for the engine's "build sheet", I was working out how to get all these engine parts to school. Finally, I got the engine delivered in sections in trash bin bags to my house and then transferred it all into one of my local authority's refuse wheelie bins.

The next morning I was in a suit and tie, dragging the bin through the streets of Castleton to school. The few cars about at that time seemed happy enough to drive around me, albeit staring a bit in the process, presumably wondering, "What's that teacher from Matthew Moss doing nicking someone's wheelie bin?"

I put the bin at the back of school, and by 9:30 a.m. the three learners had everything out and spread around. These students spent all of Monday morning on their projects, and I visited them a couple of times until break started at 10:50 a.m. A light drizzle was setting in as I went to tell them to come in for break time, but they politely refused the invitation.

What was clear was that they were in the current of a real learning flow, and had built up significant momentum. They had hypotheses in the air about which sections were going to fit where. It was absolutely intense. And how many times does our traditional timetable interrupt flow when it takes off? With myself and the head teacher watching them through the window, I left them to it, still seriously and seamlessly engaged.

The teacher goes on to describe the learning project's twists and turns, and how the students went on to learn physics principles of mechanics, gears, chemical combustion, electrical energy, and so much more, through a combination of directed instruction by the teacher and experiments created by the students, all driven by the initial exploration of assembling a car engine from parts.

Learning Project Approaches—Prescriptive and Exploratory

Learning projects can have a clearly defined outcome right from the start of the project (a *prescriptive* project) or they can be more open-ended in nature, with the desired result discovered or progressively clarified during the course of the project (an *exploratory* project).

This prescriptive versus exploratory distinction in approaches to managing learning projects is also reflected in two approaches used by professional project managers:

- Prescriptive "waterfall" project methodologies, where all the requirements are defined up front and the work efficiently "cascades" from the original set of project requirements (including an orderly change process for things that just couldn't be predicted); and
- Agile or adaptive project approaches where the end result is not completely prescribed in the project requirements, and a series of more informal small tasks or "micro-projects" are collaboratively designed, implemented, tested, and reviewed, which then leads to the next designed mini-task and the next, until the project work is completed; this agile, adaptive approach to projects is often used to produce software for online use, where requirements, user experiences, and expectations are rapidly shifting.

For learning projects, the distinction between prescriptive and exploratory projects is especially useful, as both project approaches are often used in teaching and learning, depending on the desired learning goals. If the goal is to explore a new topic or field to see what it's all about or to discover something of interest to investigate in more detail, then an exploratory approach is fitting.

If the intention is to achieve more prescribed learning outcomes by engaging students in a predesigned and well-defined project that results in specific desired knowledge and skills outcomes, then a more prescriptive project approach would be appropriate.

Many larger learning projects are composed of both exploratory and prescriptive subprojects that in combination increase the variety and depth of learning experiences for students with diverse background knowledge, learning styles, and skills.

The differences between these two sets of project approaches can be more clearly understood by identifying their respective variations of the Define, Plan, Do, and Review (Initiating, Planning, Executing & Monitoring/Controlling, and Closing) project cycle phases, as detailed in this chart:

Prescriptive Versus Explorative Learning Project Cycle Phases

Prescriptive Learning Project Cycle Phases	Learning Project Phases	Exploratory Learning Project Cycle Phases
Identify—the prescribed end result	*Define* (Initiating)	*Imagine*—the possible exploration paths and select the most promising ones
Design—the process and steps to reach the end result	*Plan* (Planning)	*Discover*—the concepts and principles of a field and possibilities for end results
Create—the end result as designed with small changes that improve the design	*Do* (Executing & Monitoring/ Controlling)	*Model*—create models (mind maps, drawings, charts, etc.) that capture your learning and are candidates for further development
Evaluate—the process, learning, and end product in meeting the requirements of the prescribed end result	*Review* (Closing)	*Evolve*—pick one or two models to fully develop into learning artifacts that best capture your learning and/ or your answers, solutions, positions, or expressions

As the project management profession moves toward more flexible, adaptive, and agile approaches to managing certain types of projects (such as internet software development), the opportunities to apply some of these proven techniques to more exploratory learning projects will grow.

Though the sharing of these agile business-oriented project methods with the world of education and schools is still in its early stages, a rich exchange between project managers and educators will likely result in broader, more inclusive approaches to effectively managing both the exploratory and prescriptive aspects of "hybrid" learning projects that better match the common twists and turns of students' rich learning journeys.

Evaluating Projects— Products, Process, and Learning Progress

How Should Learning Project Outcomes Be Evaluated?

The Three-Legged Stool of Project Evaluation

There are three important parts of effective evaluations of learning projects, pictured here as a three-legged stool:

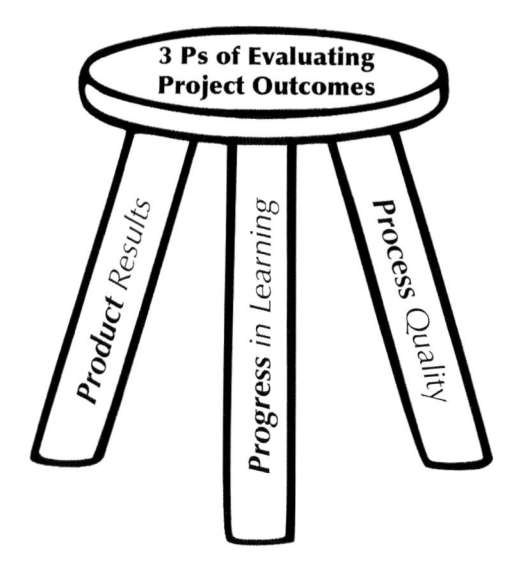

3 Ps of Evaluating Project Outcomes

Product Results

Progress in Learning

Process Quality

The Three-Legged Stool of Evaluating Project Outcomes

The three project evaluation components are:

- The quality and impact of the *product* results (a report, product, presentation, performance, model, artifact, device, program, website, etc.), and the craftsmanship of the project work that contributed to it;
- The quality and effectiveness of the project *processes* used in each phase of the project that helped produce the end results—the definition, planning, doing, and reviewing efforts of the project team, including the reviewing of the reviewing process(!); and
- The *progress* in learning outcomes for each project member and the whole team, often aligned to a set of common educational learning goals

Evaluating Product Results

In any learning project, the review process usually involves using a number of *evaluation rubrics*—sets of evaluation criteria with descriptions of each level of proficiency possible for each of the criteria, rated by both the teacher and student, often using a numerical rating for each proficiency level. Rubrics for science content, artistic design, communication skills, and creativity were used in the Blood Project described in Educator Chapter 2 for evaluating both the final exhibit and the ongoing project work.

A well-developed example of a comprehensive evaluation rubric that scores the end result of a student project to create a solution to a real-world problem is the scoring rubric used in a past international student competition called ThinkQuest, where student teams submitted a website that presents all the aspects of their problem-solving project. The program's Assessment Rubric was developed by the Oracle Education Foundation to judge student entries in its past annual global student competition, as shown on the next page.

ThinkQuest Website Evaluation Rubric

Criteria	Emerging	Developing	Accomplished	Exceptional
Critical Thinking Skills	1	2	3	4
Scope/Nature of the Problem	The problem and its solution unclear and confusing.	The problem is clear but the solution not reasonable in scope.	The problem and solution reasonable in scope and seem achievable.	The problem and solution reasonable in scope, achievable, and particularly interesting, innovative, or provocative.
Target Audience	Difficult to understand who the target audience is.	Target audience defined too broadly or not well matched to the problem.	Target audience is clear and well matched to the problem.	Target audience clear, well matched to the problem, and there's evidence that the team interacted with the audience.
The Case for the Solution	Not clear how the solution benefits the target audience.	A clear, compelling case for how the solution benefits the audience, but lacks supporting evidence or research to back the solution.	The case for the solution is compelling and cites the team's own research, or uses credible data from others to support the case for the solution.	The case for the solution is compelling, cites the team's own original research, and uses credible data from other sources to strongly support the case for the solution.
Testing and Revisions	Little indication that the team tested the solution, and no info on how the testing informed decisions.	Unclear or incomplete explanation of how the team tested the solution and how the testing informed revisions.	Clearly and completely states how the team tested the solution and how the testing informed revisions.	Clearly and completely states how the team tested the solution, how the testing informed revisions, presents unresolved issues, and offers reasons why they're unresolved or how to resolve them.
Effectiveness of the Solution	Two or more are true: * Not clear how the problem is solved. * No evidence of the solution's effectiveness. * Parts of the solution are incomplete or missing. * Not clear how the solution benefits the audience.	Only one is true: * Not clear how the problem is solved. * No evidence of the solution's effectiveness. * Parts of the solution are incomplete or missing. * Not clear how the solution benefits the audience.	How the solution solves the problem is clear and complete, there is evidence of the solution's effectiveness with the target audience, and the effectiveness of the solution is clearly and completely demonstrated.	How the solution solves the problem is clear and complete, there is evidence of the solution's effectiveness with the target audience, the effectiveness of the solution is clearly and completely demonstrated, and the team's solution provides a powerful and innovative approach to the problem, perhaps making previous solutions obsolete.
Impact on the Team	It is difficult to understand what the team learned from their description.	What the team learned is described, but is vague or incomplete.	What the team learned is completely and coherently described and includes how their learning applies to future endeavors.	What the team learned is completely and coherently described, includes how their learning applies to future endeavors, and is particularly compelling, genuine, or insightful.

(continued)

ThinkQuest Website Evaluation Rubric *(continued)*

Criteria	Emerging	Developing	Accomplished	Exceptional
Communication Skills	1	2	3	4
Content Organization and Writing Style	The content is not well organized and the writing style is inconsistent throughout.	Only one is true: * The content is well organized. * The writing style is consistent throughout.	The content is well organized and the writing style is consistent throughout.	The content is well organized, the writing style is consistent throughout, and the content is structured in a way that allows users to explore each topic or issue more deeply if desired.
Writing Conventions	Content is not clearly written and contains many grammar, punctuation, and spelling errors.	Much of the content is clearly written, but has a number of grammar, punctuation, and spelling errors.	Practically all of the content is clearly written, with only a few grammar, punctuation, and spelling errors.	All content is very polished, is clearly written, grammatically correct, with no spelling, or punctuation errors.
Plagiarism	Most text is written in students' own words or is quoted properly from cited sources, with only a few questionable areas.	All text is written in students' own words or is quoted properly from cited sources.	All text is written in students' own words or is quoted properly from cited sources, with links to the sources.	All text is written in students' own words with clear attributions to which students wrote each part, and all other nonstudent written materials are quoted properly from cited sources.
Citations and Reference List	There are no citations or the reference list is incomplete or poorly organized.	Citations/references are comprehensive, but some citations are missing or formatted inconsistently.	Citations/references are comprehensive, consistently formatted, and citations are close to the content cited.	Citations/references are comprehensive, consistently formatted, citations are close to the content cited, and the reference list indicates that sufficient research was done to support the design of the solution.
Technology Skills	1	2	3	4
Choice of Tools	The chosen tools are not the most appropriate for the content or the overall user experience.	Some tools effectively convey content and are well suited to the overall user experience.	All tools chosen effectively convey content and are well suited to the overall user experience.	All tools chosen effectively convey content and are well suited to the overall user experience, and are used in unique and creative ways to promote user interest and engagement.
Page Titles	Most of the page titles are confusing, vague, and create user frustration.	Some of the page titles are confusing or vague, requiring users to click for more info.	All page titles provide users with a clear sense of the page's content and allow users to quickly get to the content they want.	All page titles provide users with a clear sense of the page's content, allow users to quickly get to the content they want, and the navigation structure helps users stay engaged and explore more content.
Appearance	Two or more are true: * Colors interfere with viewing content. * Fonts are difficult to read. * Page layout is cluttered. * Visual elements are not suited to understanding the content.	Only one is true: * Colors interfere with viewing content. * Fonts are difficult to read. * Page layout is cluttered. * Visual elements are not suited to understanding the content.	All of the pages are visually appealing, enhance access to the content, and help create a coherent look and feel.	All of the pages are visually appealing, enhance access to the content, help create a coherent look and feel that is particularly artistic, creative, or visually appealing.

(continued)

ThinkQuest Website Evaluation Rubric *(continued)*

Criteria	Emerging	Developing	Accomplished	Exceptional
Technology Skills	**1**	**2**	**3**	**4**
Technical Performance	Two or more are true: * There are downloading and viewing issues with files, images, audio, or video elements. * At least one page does not load properly. * There is too much uploaded content or too many external links that make accessing content difficult. * There are too many pages used to deliver content.	Only one is true: * There are downloading and viewing issues with files, images, audio, or video elements, * At least one page does not load properly, * There is too much uploaded content or too many external links that make accessing content difficult, * There are too many pages used to deliver content,	All elements in the website run smoothly and promote a seamless user experience, and the number of pages used to deliver content is appropriate.	All elements in the website run smoothly and promote a seamless user experience, the number of pages used to deliver content is appropriate, and the creative use of the tools to present the problem and solution demonstrates strong technical ability.

The ThinkQuest evaluation rubric includes rating criteria for the value of the problem, the strength and creativity of the solution, the effectiveness of the communication elements in the website, and the use of technology to convey the design and details of the students' projects, organized under the headings of Critical Thinking, Communication, and Technology Skills.

Evaluating Project Processes

Evaluating the effectiveness of the project methods used in the project—the teamwork and communications; the managing of time, tasks, resources, and quality of work; the handling of risks; and the leadership skills in keeping the end result in mind throughout the project—can be done by reviewing the documents produced for each phase of the project cycle and having each team member rate how well each of the project processes in each phase went and how they could be improved, using checklists, rubrics, and/or reflective notes, as indicated here:

Project Process Reviews

Project Cycle Phases	Project Documents in the Project Portfolio	Project Methods Checklist/Ratings/Reflections
Define *(Initiating)*	*Project Definition*	Project goal met? End result completed? End result completed on time? Resources adequate? Risks managed?
	Team Agreement	Right roles for each team member? Roles performed well? Were experts, advisors, coaches used well? Communications effective? Team decisions made well? Project changes handled well? Disagreements resolved well?
Plan *(Planning)*	*Work Plan*	Major deadlines met? All project tasks completed? All project tasks on time? Work Plan changes handled well?
Do *(Executing & Monitoring/Controlling)*	*Check-in Meeting Notes*	Regular *Check-in Meetings*? Meetings well run? Quality of work good? Teamwork productive?
Review *(Closing)*	*End Results Evaluation*	End results evaluation completed? Most significant achievements? Things to improve next time?
	Learning Outcomes Evaluation	Learning outcomes evaluations completed? Most significant achievements? Most important lessons learned?
	Project Methods Evaluation	Project methods evaluation completed? Most significant achievements? Things to improve next time?

One of the most important ways that students can evaluate their project performance is to present their project work to the public—to other students, teachers, parents, community members, project professionals, business leaders, elected officials, and so on.

Exhibition nights at school, project fairs, portfolio presentations on parent nights, presentations at PMI chapter meetings or education conferences, and more, are wonderful ways for students to hone their presentation skills, receive rich feedback on their work, and most important, allow them to celebrate all the hard-won achievements in their project work.

Celebrating the completion of projects is an essential part of the Review phase of the learning project cycle that provides an opportunity for students to take pride in their project work, receive recognition for their accomplishments, and increase their motivation to jump into the next project.

Evaluating Learning Progress

To review and evaluate each team member's *learning outcomes*, a wealth of educational methods can be used during the course of a project (*formative* evaluations) as well as at the end of a project (*summative* evaluations).

Current formative evaluation methods, which may use scoring rubrics (like the Thinkquest example above), and are often done online, include:

- Student reports and essays submitted online and scored with online rubrics;
- Observation of skills performance, with scoring rubrics on a handheld device;
- Online instant polls, quizzes, voting, and blog commentaries;
- Evaluations of current project work and mid-project reviews using online rubrics;
- Progress tracked through solving online simulations, games, and design challenges; and
- Employer evaluations of ongoing internship and service work in the community.

Modern summative evaluation methods aim to go beyond the testing of facts and basic skills in simple "fill-in-the-bubble" tests to evaluate a combination of content knowledge, basic skills, higher-order thinking skills, deeper comprehension and understanding, applied knowledge, and 21st century skills performance.

Here is an example of a summative test item that moves in this direction, evaluating critical thinking, math reasoning, visual literacy, and political and citizenship content understanding, all in one test item, from an 11th-grade state social studies assessment test in West Virginia:

Grade 11–Citizenship

SS.0.11.01.03 **analyze** the changing nature of civic responsibility

Depth of knowledge 3

Directions: The mayor of your town was asked to speak at a school assembly on citizenship. As part of her presentation, she shared the following charts and information with the eleventh graders at your school. Based on her presentation, fill in the circle next to the best answer for **Question 8**.

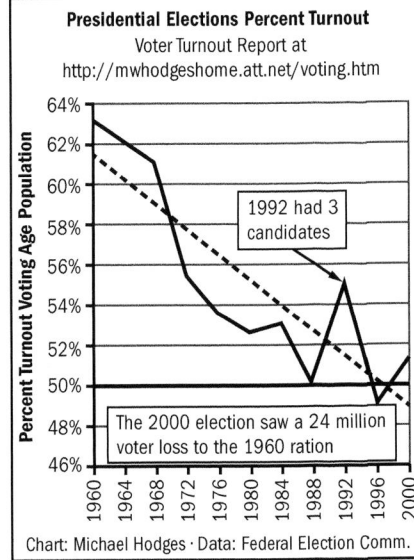

Presidential Elections Percent Turnout
Voter Turnout Report at
http://mwhodgeshome.att.net/voting.htm

1992 had 3 candidates

The 2000 election saw a 24 million voter loss to the 1960 ration

Chart: Michael Hodges · Data: Federal Election Comm.

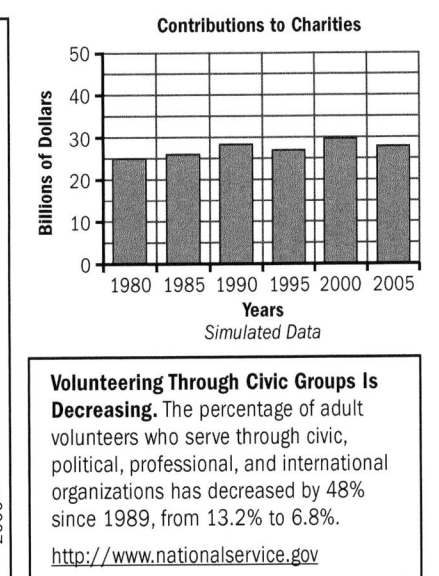

Contributions to Charities

Years
Simulated Data

Volunteering Through Civic Groups Is Decreasing. The percentage of adult volunteers who serve through civic, political, professional, and international organizations has decreased by 48% since 1989, from 13.2% to 6.8%.

http://www.nationalservice.gov

Question 8: Which of the following hypotheses would best introduce an analysis of the above data?

Ⓐ All forms of civic participation have shown a considerable decline.

Ⓑ Even though the amounts of charitable giving have held fairly consistent, civic engagement in other areas has shown a significant decrease.

Ⓒ Civic participation requiring an individual's time is more prevalent than passive participation.

Ⓓ No conclusions can be drawn from the data presented.

Example Summative Evaluation of Knowledge and Skills

Both formative and summative evaluations are often aligned to a set of core learning standards, which detail what a student should know and be able to do at each grade level in a variety of subject areas. This alignment of learning outcomes with learning standards is an important part of assessing whether a student is on track for success in primary and secondary school, is ready for postsecondary education, and has accumulated the skills and expertise to successfully enter the workforce in a job or career.

Another important evaluation method for both formative and summative assessments is taking the time for each student to write a short reflection about what has been learned in the course of a project and at the completion of the *Do (Executing & Monitoring/Controlling)* phase of a project, noting thoughts, feelings, and perspectives in a personal journal or reflection notebook.

These "thinking about thinking" activities, or "metacognitive" exercises, are very important for the development of self-understanding and self-direction, and are especially important for getting a sense of the continuous progress being made in mastering skills and building expertise. Seeing how one can do something now in a project that was virtually impossible before boosts self-confidence and fuels the desire to learn more and become even more capable and empowered.

The art and science of measuring learning progress is rapidly evolving, though education systems have been slow to adopt these new methods. The progress can be viewed as a movement from evaluations *OF* learning, to evaluations *FOR* learning, to evaluations *AS* learning:

Evaluations *OF* Learning	Evaluations *FOR* Learning	Evaluations *AS* Learning
Usually summative recall or simple demonstrations of basic skills measuring whether students have recently developed knowledge, skills, and other competencies compared to established standards, benchmarks, and learning goals * Example: *US NAEP Test*	Formative and some portfolio summative methods of identifying student learning progress in ongoing work and performance tasks, new learning needs as they arise, and opportunities to revise work and improve competencies * Example: *Performance task*	Mostly formative, meaningful learning tasks with embedded evaluations that provide immediate feedback as part of the ongoing learning experience, with a progression of challenges for increasing mastery and a wide variety of helpful feedback * Example: *Online learning game*

The Future of Project Management in Education

Project Management as a Bridge to 21ˢᵗ Century Education

Conclusions to books, like the end of projects, are often two things at once: looking back from the end of one journey and looking forward to the beginning of another.

Endings involve both rational and emotional reflections on past work done and the future work to come. And like good project reviews, they can be very personal, revealing sometimes difficult, and often deep, lessons learned.

This is author Bernie's personal concluding thoughts and feelings:

My journey to find and build crucial project bridges to 21ˢᵗ century learning has been an exciting, decade-long personal learning adventure for me—a learning project whose first complete "bridge-building" project cycle is now coming to a close, just as a new project cycle of even more and stronger bridges, with broader and deeper impacts, is starting.

Since my first meeting with Jim Snyder and others from PMI and PMIEF well over a decade ago, I knew my hunch was right that what PBL and deeper learning methods were missing to become a truly global force for shifting how students learn in school, at

home, and in the community could be found somewhere in the collective wisdom of the project management profession.

At the time, I thought all it would take was a little adapting of the language and methods of project management (as captured in the profession's "Bible"—the infamous PMBOK Guide *or Project Management Body of Knowledge) for the world of education and PBL to become project management–savvy. The key formula would be:*

PM + PBL = 21st Century Learning for Career, Community, and Life

Little did I know the depth of the challenges involved (for both project management professionals and educators) in taking a highly developed business and technical language and a set of well-honed and deep project methodologies and translating them for education audiences, who rarely knew much about the project management profession, and had little, if any, exposure to project management methods in their entire education career!

In the early days of my work with PMIEF, *when asking large groups of educators (even those very familiar with PBL) whether they knew much about the field of project management or personally knew of a real project manager, only a few hands, if any, would go up.*

With teachers who were well experienced in PBL methods with their students, when I asked what some of the biggest challenges were in doing effective PBL, a very frequent response was "being able to better manage multiple projects, and having students become much better at managing their own projects activities—especially managing time, deadlines, and teamwork."

Also in those early days when I asked large groups of professional project managers if they would like their own children to learn the fundamentals of project management at school and in community projects, virtually all hands would go up!

When I asked if they would be willing to volunteer some of their time to help teachers and their students get better at doing and managing their learning projects, a very high percentage would raise their hands, often adding the well-considered caveat that they would do it if they were given some helpful training about the current world of students, classrooms, and teachers doing learning

projects, and could be versed in the classroom practices that teachers and students often experience in their learning projects.

So, the bridge-building between project management and school learning project approaches began with high expectations and strong motivations from both PMs and educators.

A decade later, so much has been learned and so much has been developed (and redeveloped from feedback) to help educators and project managers work together to build the skills, understandings, and mindsets that students now need to be successful.

This book is one of many resources now available from PMIEF to help make the "project management of learning projects" a whole lot clearer, with lots of useful tools, templates, and examples for both teachers and students to follow as they define, plan, do, and review their learning projects.

What were some of the important lessons learned along the bridge-building journey to "PM + PBL = 21ˢᵗ Century Learning?" Here are a few key ones:

- *Once educators are exposed to the project cycle phases (often a new concept for them) and the idea that there are certain activities specific to each phase that really promote overall project success, things get a lot clearer; they have a new framework for thinking about how projects really work.*
- *The most crucial part of any project is communications— clear, frequent, and simply structured, open communications on what's happening in each phase of a project among all the team members (leveraging social media and collaboration tools is especially helpful here).*
- *The more time spent in the* Define (Initiating) *and* Plan (Planning) *phases of a learning project, with plenty of time to research and review what each person is learning about the project challenge and plenty of time to "refine the define and the design" of what's going to be done in the project, the more likely the project will be successful.*
- *Very few projects are ever done entirely from the first plan— things will change, and change can often be your best friend in coming up with a better project outcome, if everyone clearly understands what the changes are and what they will be doing differently from the previous plan.*

- *Giving students opportunities to present their project work to the public, including experts in the topic areas of their projects, with time for rich discussions of the projects, what was learned, how the project process went, how they could improve the quality of the results, and what they want to learn next, all based on their project experiences, is essential to motivation, learning, and building public-speaking skills that may be the key to future success in work and community life.*
- *The most important of all the lessons learned is: In all learning projects, it's the* learning *that always counts the most! Even if a project is not fully completed or is abandoned for a new and different project that is better suited for highly motivated learning, as long as the learning is deep, rich, and exciting, the project can be considered successful.*

Looking toward the future of project management in education, there are a number of very hopeful signs that the "PM + PBL = 21st Century Learning" bridges will continue to transform teaching and learning practices so that all students are better prepared for their futures. There are also some wonderful connections with similar project learning processes from other areas of education and learning, including the following:

- *It is becoming quite clear that the world of work is increasingly a project world—projects may be the most common unit of work in the future. Starting early in primary school and refining one's project skills may be the key to reversing a disturbingly high level of un- and underemployment among the world's youth.*
- *The growing need for STEM/DREAMS job skills further highlights the importance of project competence, as much of the work in these areas is highly project oriented.*
- *Frameworks for Engineering, Design Thinking & Doing, the Maker Movement, PBL, and other real-world challenge-based efforts easily map to project management's project cycle, making project competence an even more valuable and unifying complement (see the comparison chart of some of these other processes in Project Learning Resources—Project Method Framework Comparisons on page 98).*

- *An important part of current efforts to better define high-quality PBL involves a more thorough integration of project management methods with the best practices of PBL—collaboration between PMIEF and the Buck Institute for Education on this important challenge is currently under way.*
- *Social media and online collaboration tools on smartphones are making the managing of projects more visual, more social, more motivating, and more fun for students to stay engaged and communicating throughout their projects. We can expect more comprehensive, visually intuitive, and highly integrated tools and apps for managing learning projects throughout the project cycle phases to be developed in the future.*
- *Look to more micro-credentials, badging, and certifications for project management skill development that recognize and reward developed project management competencies, by digitally submitting project work and portfolios, all done online.*
- *Because students often are in an exploratory mode in their learning before defining a more detailed learning project, and because exploratory projects are very much like agile projects, there is much more work to be done in translating what has been learned in professional agile project management practices that could apply to these exploratory learning projects.*
- *As education moves toward equipping students with the skills and social/emotional competencies needed in a more project world, group learning projects offer wonderful opportunities for students to learn and practice techniques for developing their social and emotional skills such as teamwork, empathy, curiosity, courage, persistence, resilience, leadership, and ethical behavior.*
- *It is becoming much clearer that helping students "learn how to learn" and be more self-propelled, self-managing learners with a wide range of learning strategies that often match the practices learned in projects may be the most important set of skills a student can develop for a lifetime of learning and motivated work.*

In many ways, the project cycle is really a learning *cycle—defining what one wants to learn, planning how to learn it, researching and building the skills needed to develop deeper understanding and competence,*

and frequently reviewing where one is in the learning process and where to go next.

As we look to the future we can easily say:

> *Learning is our most vital lifelong project,*
> *and learning how to navigate and manage our learning*
> *may be the most essential of all the 21st century skills—*
> *learning how to be a self-propelled, lifelong learner.*

May all your future projects be exciting adventures across bridges to new landscapes of exploration, discovery, and the joy of learning!

Project Bridges to 21st Century Learning

A Learning Project Sampler

This section features three real-life learning projects done in schools around the globe, where a professional project manager and a teacher (or teachers) worked together to provide 21st century learning experiences for students—bridges successfully built between education and project management!

The projects are sequenced by grade level—from the youngest students to the oldest, from elementary to middle to secondary school student projects. They feature the exemplary project methods used in each of the project cycle phases. (Some of these projects are also described in the *PMIEF/P21 Skills Map—Project Management for Learning*, available at http://www.p21.org/storage/documents/Skills/Skills%20Map/Project_Management_Skills_Map_Final.pdf)

The format for each project includes the following:

- *Project Intro*—brief background "story" of the project

- *Project Description*
  - ○ Project Goals
  - ○ Project Types (Inquiry, Design, Debate, Expression)
  - ○ Subject Areas (Language arts, Science, Arts and design, Technology skills, etc.)
  - ○ Related Career Pathways (Energy, Arts and media, Information technology, etc.)
- *Project Cycle Activities by Phase*—Define (Initiating), Plan (Planning), Do (Executing & Monitoring/Controlling), Review (Closing)
  - ○ Activities and Tools
  - ○ Project Work Examples
  - ○ 21st Century Skills Developed (see Project Learning Resources—21st Century Skills Descriptions on pages 90–97)

As a helpful summary reference guide to the project examples, a brief review of the key roles and project phases used in each of the projects is outlined in Learning Resources, Key Learning Project Components Review (green tabbed section) on pages 82-87.

Primary Grades 3–5: Art Exhibition Project

PROJECT INTRO

Students in an elementary school in Milan, Italy, planned, organized, and ran a large exhibition of student portfolios of art, showing the development of artistic and project skills across grades 3, 4, and 5.

Students planned and designed the exhibition space, designed and created the invitations to the exhibition and a web page to advertise the event, and on the exhibition night, explained their art projects to parents, community members, and other students. They also ran a sale of homemade artistic "gadgets" to raise funds for a local charity.

As an additional outcome, their collaborative experience validated the project management toolkit conceived by the joint team of school teachers and chapter volunteers.

The Project Management Toolkit for Primary Schools was Used and Validated Through the Student Work

Primary Grades 3–5: Art Exhibition Project

PROJECT DESCRIPTION

Project Goals

- To showcase the developing creative and expressive skills of each student in a gallery-like showcase event

- To develop the project management skills of students in planning, designing, and running the art exhibition

- To develop the technical communication and reflection skills of students as they present their project work to the public and advertise the event on the web

- To develop student entrepreneurial and marketing skills through raising money for local charities by selling small pieces of student artwork—"gadgets"

Project Types

- Design
- Expression

Subject Areas

- Art and design
- Language arts
- Technology skills

Related Career Pathways

- Arts and media
- Information technology
- Marketing and sales

DEFINE (Initiating) PHASE

In their *Brainstorming* and *Mind Mapping* project activities, the students outlined all the things that needed to be done to have a successful art exhibition and sale, from choosing the artwork to be displayed, to advertising and inviting attendees to the exhibition.

They used yellow stickies on a chart to capture all the brainstormed activities, then organized them into a structured mindmap under the basic categories: Why?, What?, Who?, Where?, When?, and What if?, as shown here:

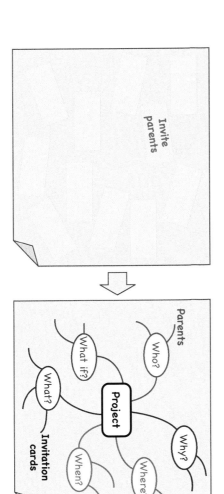

Primary Grades 3–5: Art Exhibition Project

PLAN (Planning) PHASE

In developing the *Activity Tree* and the *Project Calendar*, the students organized and sequenced all the tasks necessary for project success, assigned deadlines and owners for the tasks, and mapped out the workflow for the entire project.

With the *Activity Tree* chart, the students sorted the yellow stickies developed in the previous brainstorming activity under major activity categories and subcategories, creating a "tree" of related project activities, as shown here:

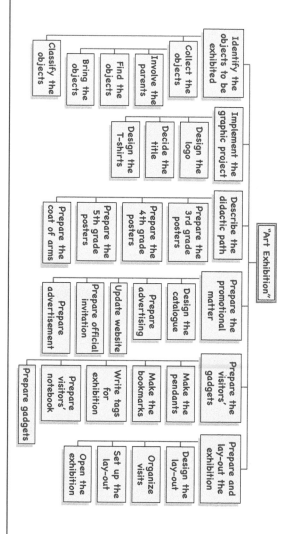

DO (Executing & Monitoring/Controlling) PHASE

As the work proceeded with getting all the art exhibits ready, sending out invitations, organizing the layout of the exhibition, considering the best way to make the experiences flow for the attendees, how the "gadget" sale should be organized and run, etc., the students found that parts of their activity plan and calendar needed adjustments.

The students used a weekly *Traffic Light-colored Faces* chart to indicate how each of the calendar activities were doing—green happy faces for "it's OK, keep on going", yellow/orange concerned faces for "watch out", and red sad faces for "stop, this needs attention right away".

The *Project Traffic Light Faces* helped the students reprioritize their work and see that certain critical resources (like more tablecloths for the exhibit tables, a better way to deal with cash sales at the gadget table, adjustments to the plan when a student was absent, etc.) had to be addressed to keep the project on schedule and ready for the opening evening of the exhibition.

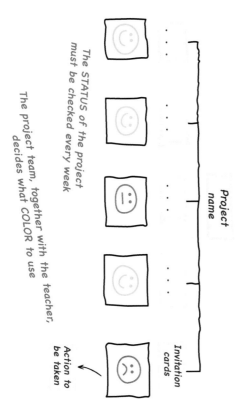

Project name

Invitation cards

Action to be taken

The STATUS of the project must be checked every week

The project team, together with the teacher, decides what COLOR to use

REVIEW (Closing) PHASE

Each student created a *Lessons Learned* chart (shown below) that answered the following questions:

- What new things did I learn?
- What was the most difficult thing?
- What was the most enjoyable part?
- What would I change for next time?
- What could I have done better?

This led to the sharing of each of the students' charts and some additional reflections, as well as a party celebration for a project well done!

Middle Grades 6–10: Olympic Stadium Design Project

PROJECT INTRO

Recognizing that all students need to be 21st century learners equipped with life, learning, and career skills that will prepare them for further studies and their future careers, Mill Chase Community Technology College, a Hampshire (United Kingdom) secondary school for students 11–16 years old, embarked on a program to help students learn the essentials of managing and leading real-world projects.

With support from project managers in the PMI local chapter and education consultants, a pilot program was launched with the 11-year-old students and their teachers, the first in a series of projects being a team challenge to design a world-class stadium for the then-upcoming London 2012 Olympics.

Students working on Olympic Stadium Project

PROJECT DESCRIPTION

Project Goals

- To develop a winning stadium design for the 2012 London Olympics and Paralympics
- To demonstrate how the design will continue to benefit the local community and the country after the Olympics
- To present and defend the design before a panel of judges

Project Types

- Design
- Inquiry

Subject Areas

- Sports and physical education
- Architecture, art, and design
- Science and engineering
- Math
- Language arts
- Technology skills

Related Career Pathways

- Building and environmental design
- Engineering
- Hospitality and tourism
- Marketing and sales
- Information technology

Middle Grades 6–10: Olympic Stadium Design Project

DEFINE (Initiating) PHASE

Prior to the start of the project, the project teachers engaged in an in-depth training with PMI project managers and educational consultants, experiencing all phases of the project cycle as they learned about key methods and tools to help manage the moving parts of each project phase.

Acting as the project client, the teacher introduced the *Project Brief* that briefly described the aims and requirements of the Olympic stadium design competition.

The student teams then responded to the aims and requirements in the *Project Brief* with their initial ideas for a solution in a project scope statement (what the project will do and what it won't do) and then outlined the project deliverables—their designs, models, presentations, etc.—that they would develop as part of the project.

The students also filled out a *Stakeholders Table* that identified each person with a key interest in the project, her/his role, what the stakeholder wanted from the project team, and how the team planned on giving stakeholders what they needed.

Finally, each project team summarized the entire definition of the project, its scope, stakeholders, and deliverables, in a presentation and discussion with the client (the teacher or business member), ending with a formal signing by all the team members and the client of the final *Client Agreement* document.

Students Reviewing Project Plans

PLAN (Planning) PHASE

The Planning Phase involved in a number of project team activities, including creating the following:

- A *Work Breakdown Structure (WBS)*—breaking down what needs doing into manageable work chunks, as in this sample *Activity Tree* diagram:

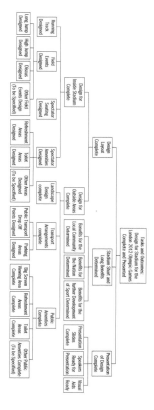

- A *Project Schedule*—often done in an electronic project schedule format such as a Gantt chart or flow map outlining each task in sequence, start and end dates, and required resources for each task.

- A *Risks List* for the project —where things could likely go wrong and what could be done to minimize the chance that those risks would happen (often adjusting the Project Schedule to hedge against the risks), and if they did happen, what "Plan B" (and C and D) would look like.

- *Work Packages*—breaking down the larger-scale WBS into tasks for which each team member will be responsible, the sequence in which the tasks should be done, estimates for how long each task will take, which resources will be needed, when must each task be done, etc.

The final step in the Planning Phase is to get the "go-ahead" from the client to continue on to the next phase of the project cycle.

Middle Grades 6–10: Olympic Stadium Design Project

DO (Executing & Monitoring/Controlling) Phase

The Do Phase is where the research, design, graphics, documents, diagrams, models, presentation slides, presentation practicing, and so on were all accomplished—where the real work of fulfilling the project plan, creating the design solutions, and preparing to present the results were done. It is important in this phase to continually *Track Progress*, monitor the quality of all project artifacts and deliverables, communicate and collaborate across the team and with the stakeholders, adjust the schedule and work plan as needed, and note lessons learned along the way.

To track progress, project teams filled out a Status Report at the end of each week of the project, answering questions such as these:

- Is the project going according to plan? Why or why not?

- Do you need to make any changes to the plan?

- What do you have to do next in the project?

- Does everyone know what's going on, what to do, and when?

- Is what is being produced going to please the client? Is the quality good?

- What lessons have you recently learned from doing this project?

To effectively communicate the design solutions and present highlights of the project work that each team has accomplished, effort was put into developing *Presentation Skills*, with time to practice and receive coaching before making the final presentations to the judges and the attending audience.

Boys Working on Learning Project

REVIEW (Closing) PHASE

The students' design solutions were presented to a panel of judges, who scored each team on their design, skills learned, project management skills, and presentation factors. Here are the criteria (they also had scoring scales for each criteria) the judges used to score each team's project work:

- Design fit to needs, quality, and creativity of pro-posed solution
- Evidence of desired skills learned in the project
  - o Research and inquiry skills
  - o Teamwork, leadership, and participation skills
  - o Self-management and self-direction skills
  - o Self-reflection and self-correcting skills
  - o Creative thinking and doing skills
- Evidence of understanding and application of good project management principles and practices
- Presentation skills
  - o Structure and organization of ideas and content
  - o Delivery—clear speaking, connecting with audi-ence, answering questions well, etc.
  - o Effective use of visual media and physical models
  - o Teamwork in group presentations

Each teacher and student provided an overall evaluation of the entire project so that the lessons learned could be ap-plied to future project in other grades and in other schools.

Some of the areas indicated for improvement included the need to start with simpler, shorter projects and work up to a more complex one; further simplification of project termi-nology for young students; more time for teacher develop-ment; more practice using project tools and templates; and more student work time and teacher collaboration time.

Each student received a Project Completion Certificate in a celebratory ceremony:

Children Celebrating the End of the Olympic Project

PROJECT DESCRIPTION

Project Goals

- To gain both academic knowledge and hands-on, applied, technical expertise in:
  - Engineering design
  - 3-D CAD design
  - Digital electronics design
  - Aerospace engineering
  - Robotics design
- To have multiple opportunities to learn and practice project management and leadership methods in their work
- To be able to apply both technical and project management expertise to projects in other non-CTE classes in high school and in the community

Project Types

- Design
- Inquiry

Subject Areas

- Science and engineering
- Math
- 3-D design
- Project management
- Digital electronics
- Aerospace engineering
- Robotics
- Information technology

- Engineering
- Information technology
- Manufacturing
- Transportation

The class was led by Karl Ruff who is a Career and Technical Education (CTE) Teacher Roosevelt High School in Seattle, WA, USA. He is pictured here.

Karl Ruff, Washington State Career and Technical Education (CTE) Teacher

DEFINE (Initiating) PHASE

Students spend the first semester of their CTE project acquiring background knowledge, building small components that can be used in their second semester project, mastering skills on the equipment they will use in constructing their designs, and making plans for their second semester master project.

The first semester is fairly prescriptive, with optional activities that allow students to explore areas of greater interest.

The second semester is devoted to constructing their designs for a device that incorporates virtually everything that they have learned in the first semester, and students regularly present their designs to their classmates as shown here:

All of these project activities are spelled out in the *Project Definitions* for the different CTE courses.

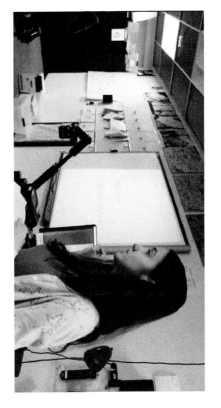

Student Presenting Team's Learning Project to the Class

Each of the CTE courses is modularized and self-paced so students can work at their own speed in learning and developing skills in each subject area.

To help the teacher and students manage the many projects all going on at the same time, a *Project Charter*, a *Project Organization Chart*, a *Visual WBS (Work Breakdown Structure) Diagram*, and a *Project Schedule Gantt Chart* for each project is always visible on one wall of the classroom, and these are updated regularly to show where each project and its team members are in the flow of project activities as shown here:

Student Showing Work Breakdown Structure and Project Plan

Student project managers hold weekly *Project Status Meetings*, which includes updates on the work tasks listed in the *Visual WBS Diagram*, and a review and update of the *Project Schedule* to adjust timelines and preview upcoming tasks. This weekly "glue" that holds the projects together gives everyone a chance to evaluate how things are going, prepare for what's coming, and make sure everyone knows what's going on in each project. It also provides opportunities for students to exercise their communication, collaboration, and negotiation skills.

The *Project Status Meetings* also provide a safe place to air small and large shortcomings and challenges, get help from other project team members, and learn from others how to improve project skills. Two of Karl Ruff's students are discussing the latest challenges they face in their projects:

Students Reviewing Project Plans

REVIEW (Closing) PHASE

Both an individual *Project Review* with each student and a team project review with the whole team, led by the team's student project manager, are used to evaluate and assess the achievements of each project team. Karl doing an individual *Project Review* with a student is shown here:

At the end of the second semester, each project team demonstrates the device they created for their chosen course project at a *Project Exhibition*:

- A taffy-pulling machine for engineering design
- A T-shirt printer for robotics
- A remote-controlled dirigible for aerospace engineering
- A school emergency exit sign for digital electronics design
- A T-shirt cannon launcher for 3-D design

Karl Ruff Reviewing Project With Student

Some of the questions used for the project review include:

- Were the project goals met and the end result completed on time?
- Were the resources and research support adequate?
- Were the right roles assigned for each team member and did each member perform well?
- Were outside experts, advisors, or information sources used well?

- Was team communication effective?
- Were the team decisions made well?
- Were project changes handled well?
- Were disagreements resolved well?
- What were the most significant achievements, both individually and as a group?
- What would make an even better project next time?
- What were the most important lessons learned?

Key Learning Project Components Review

Project Learning Players and Roles

These days, it often takes a team (and sometimes a village) to get projects in gear and successfully completed.

As work and learning become more complex, more information- and technology-rich, and more connected to entire worlds of knowledge and expertise, projects need a team approach to pool diverse talents and collectively come up with sound answers to perplexing questions, innovative solutions to thorny problems, persuasive arguments for a controversial position, or inspirational works of expressive power.

This is also true for learning projects, which often tackle important questions, problems, issues, and expressions, giving students opportunities to develop and apply essential skills to real-world and real-life situations, making their learning more relevant and memorable.

Though each project has its own particular requirements for the kinds of talent and expertise needed for success, a long history of project management experience has shown that certain project roles are important to include for the successful managing and leading of projects in general, and for learning projects in particular.

The key project learning players and their roles are listed here:

Project Players and Roles

Project Learning Players	Project Learning Roles
Project Champion [A Sponsor in professional business projects]	The person who initiates the idea for the project and/or is highly motivated to see it happen, who gains commitment from those who have the authority to make the project happen, and ensures that the project has the resources it needs to be successful
Project Manager	The person responsible for making sure the project meets its goals, the teamwork is productive, and team members achieve their learning goals; teachers often play this role, in student-centered learning approaches, students often take on this role or share it with the teacher(s)
Project Team Members	The persons who work with the project manager to carry out all the project activities, dividing up project tasks among them and collaborating to increase the productivity, quality, and creativity of the project work, with team members regularly reporting their progress to the project manager and one another
Project Advisors/ Coaches	Persons with expertise helpful to the project's success, such as project management professionals, subject matter experts, business leaders, elected officials, parents, etc.; they can be advisors and coaches to the teacher, the student teams, or both
Project Evaluators	Persons responsible for evaluating the quality of the project work; the effectiveness of the project's management, leadership, and teamwork, as well as the learning gains for each student and the project teams as a whole; could be the teacher, student (self-evaluation), or multiple evaluators, including other teachers, parents, advisors/coaches, community members, or other students

It's important that all the players in a project continually communicate and coordinate their work throughout all the phases of the project cycle, but more important, it is crucial for all the players to fully understand the definition of the project and its goals right at the beginning of a project.

Define (Initiating) Phase: Project Definition and Teamwork Agreement

At the beginning of a learning project, there are two resources that are particularly helpful in making sure everyone understands what the project is all about, what is expected of each player, what the intended outcomes of the project will be, and how the project team members will work together on the project—the *Project Definition* document and the *Teamwork Agreement*.

The *Project Definition* document records the answers to the key questions that define the main characteristics of the project, such as this "Defining Dozen" list of questions:

1. *Why* is this project needed?
2. *What* is this project about? (a brief description)

3. *What* is the *goal* of this project?
4. *What* will the end results of the project be? (the "deliverables" in business terms)
5. *What* will this project *not do*, even if it could be done easily?
6. *What type* of project is this? (inquiry, design, debate, expression; prescriptive or exploratory; or a combination)
7. *What* is the driving *question*, *problem*, *issue*, or *perspective* that motivates the work in this project?
8. *When* will the project need to be completed?
9. *Where* will the project be done?
10. *What* resources are needed to successfully complete the project? (equipment, tools, materials, funding, technology, online resources, books, etc.)
11. *How* will the project be evaluated? (quality of the project work and end results, the learning outcomes, the effectiveness of the project methods)
12. *What* risks are involved in the project? (events or conditions that may delay or impact project work)

All of the answers to *Who*-related teamwork questions are often recorded in another document, called the *Teamwork Agreement:*

- Who will be involved in the project, and what is each person's *role or roles?*

- What are each team member's *strengths, expertise,* and *preferences?*

- How and how often will the project team *communicate with one another?*

- How will outside experts, coaches, and advisors be used in the project?

- How will *decisions* be made?

- How will project *changes* be handled?

- How will *disagreements* be resolved?

With the increasing diversity of student backgrounds, perspectives, and personalities now in our schools and communities, the positive handling of disagreements and conflicting opinions is of particular importance to effective teamwork and project success.

Understanding that each person may have a different approach to handling conflict—that each person may have different levels of assertiveness and cooperativeness that lead to differing behaviors such as avoiding, accommodating, compromising, competing and collaborating—can help in developing more sensitive and positive approaches to resolving issues, as the following *Five Styles of Handling Conflict* chart from *Educators for Social Responsibility* illustrates:

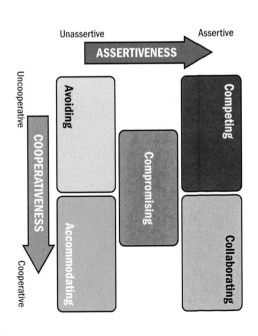

Five Styles of Handling Conflict from *Educators for Social Responsibility*

It's important that the understandings and promises outlined in the *Teamwork Agreement* are fully acceptable to every member of the project team. It can be helpful if all the team members put their personal signatures on the document to indicate their commitment to following the teamwork guidelines and processes included in the agreement.

These two documents and the *Work Plan* described below are often combined into one project document, sometimes called a "Project Brief" or "Project Charter" or just the *Project Portfolio*, which becomes a constant companion to the project team members and is referred to frequently and updated as needed during the course of a project.

85

Plan (Planning) Phase: The Work Plan

In the second phase of the learning project cycle—the Plan Phase—organizing and planning out the team members' project work is the focus. It is most helpful at this phase to collaboratively develop a *Work Plan* document that includes items such as:

- A list of project *deadlines* for each phase of the project work (when each of the Define, Plan, Do, and Review phases should be completed);

- A list of project *tasks* in the order they need to be performed;

- The project *owners* for each of the tasks;

- The *resources* needed for each task (materials, tools, funding, expert advice, etc.); and

- *Time schedules* for each of the tasks (start and finish dates).

There is a wide variety of templates and tools available, both paper- and software-based, that help learning project managers and team members in their planning, scheduling, and managing of the project tasks and activities.

These range from a simple project "to-do" checklist that lists all the tasks in the order they are to be accomplished (and checked off as they are completed), to sophisticated project management software applications that help track each project task, who owns each task, what resources are needed to accomplish each task, the estimated and actual time to complete the task, which tasks are dependent on others being completed, if the work submitted is of acceptable quality or needs further revisions, which tasks are the most critical to meet the deadlines, and much more.

In prescriptive projects, especially complex ones, closely following a *Work Plan* is essential to project success. In more exploratory projects, the scheduling of specific tasks can be much more flexible, particularly in the early phases. As the project progresses and the desired end results become clearer, a *Work Plan* can be very useful in reaching the goals and timeline for the project.

Continuously updating a *Work Plan* as the project moves through the Do Phase is often a real challenge. This job is frequently the responsibility of the project manager, though with collaborative online project tools it is increasingly possible for the project team members to update their own progress and see what all the other team members are accomplishing as the project moves forward.

Do (Executing & Monitoring/Closing) Phase: Check-in Meetings

Once the team members have entered the Do Phase of the project cycle, three important considerations move to the top of the list of project managing concerns:

- Are team members consistently meeting the expectations set in the *Work Plan*, and if not, can the *Work Plan* be modified without putting the whole project at risk?

- Is the *quality of work* meeting the needs of the project, or must time be taken to improve or redo the work?

- Is the *communication* among team members sufficient to help keep things on track and to see how all the parts of the project are working together?

Team communications are crucial in this phase, and regular *Check-in Meetings* (face-to-face or virtual), led by the project manager or one of the team members, are essential for making sure the other two concerns—following the *Work Plan* and producing the quality of work needed in the project—are being carefully monitored and any issues that need attention are taken care of.

Check-in Meetings can be as simple as having project team members briefly share their answers to the following four questions, with the project manager or a team member taking notes to be added to the Do section of the *Project Portfolio*:

1. What have you completed recently?
2. What are you working on now?
3. When do you think the current task will be done?
4. What do you need to keep your work on track with good quality?

Occasionally (and possibly more often than we'd like to admit), it becomes clear from these meetings that a major change to the *Work Plan*, or even to the *Project Definition*, must be made. At this point, the project manager and a selection of team members must take the time to adjust or redo the definition and planning documents, and then hold a lengthier meeting to update everyone on the project changes.

To keep the quality of the project work at the level needed to successfully complete the project, it is helpful to have evaluation criteria for each of the major pieces of project work produced and for the desired end results. This leads to the Review Phase of the learning project cycle.

Though project monitoring and reviewing is an important ongoing activity in all the other learning project phases (the real-time "cyclometer" readings in the project cycle

model), the Review Phase is where full attention is focused on evaluating, and celebrating, the achievements of the entire project.

There are three project outcomes that need to be reviewed in this phase:

- The quality and impact of the *product results* (a report, product, presentation, performance, model, artifact, device, program, website, etc.) and the craftsmanship of the key project work that contributed to it;

- The *progress in learning outcomes* for each project member and the whole team, often aligned to a set of common educational learning goals; and

- The quality and effectiveness of the *project processes* used in each phase of the project that helped produce the end results—the definition, planning, doing, and reviewing efforts of the project team, including reviewing the reviewing process.

Project Management Pathways

Learning how to manage and lead effective projects can follow a variety of pathways, often starting simply and moving along a trajectory toward a more professional approach to project management and leadership.

The development of project management and leadership skills can start very early in life as a set of simple life skills that help get things done, move on to a more detailed and rigorous approach with learning projects and mastering project learning skills, then continue the trajectory to a career or professional project management approach as practiced by project managers in every field of work, as shown in this pathways chart:

Project Management Pathways

Life Skills →	Learning Skills →	Career Skills →
Project Steps (Four Steps)	**Project Cycle** (Four Phases)	**Project Methodology** (Five Processes)*
• Set a Goal • Plan the Steps • Do It • Review It	• Define • Do • Review	• Initiating • Planning • Executing • Monitoring & Controlling • Closing
	Prescriptive • Identify • Design • Create • Evaluate	Exploratory • Imagine • Discover • Model • Evolve	Agile-Adaptive • Envision • Speculate • Explore • Adapt • Close

* From: *A Guide to the Project Management Book of Knowledge (PMBOK® Guide)* – Six Edition

(continued)

Project Management Pathways (continued)

Life Skills →	Learning Skills →	Career Skills →
Project Methods	**Project Methods**	**Project Methods**

Goal Setting
- Project Size
- Project Quality

Step Planning
- Steps Sequence
- Time
- Resources
- Team Roles

Troubleshooting and Fixing

Project Definition
- Project and Learning Goals
- Learning Project Type
- End Results
- Driving Question, Problem, Issue, Perspective
- Completion Date
- Needed Resources
- Evaluation Methods
- Project Risks

Team Agreement
- Team Roles
- Team Member Profiles
- Communication Methods
- Decision-Making Methods
- Disagreement Resolution Methods
- Change Management

Work Plan
- Project Deadlines
- Project Tasks
- Task Owners
- Resources Needed
- Time Schedules

Check-in Meetings
- Work Plan Progress
- Quality of Work
- Communication Effectiveness

Evaluations
- End Results
- Learning Outcomes
- Project Methods

Knowledge Areas
- Scope
- Time
- Cost
- Quality
- Teamwork
- Communications
- Risk
- Resources
- Integration

P21 Framework for 21st Century Learning
21st Century Student Outcomes and Support Systems

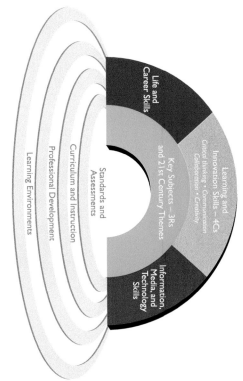

Life and Career Skills

Learning and Innovation Skills – 4Cs
Critical thinking • Communication
Collaboration • Creativity

Key Subjects – 3Rs and 21st Century Themes

Information, Media, and Technology Skills

Standards and Assessments

Curriculum and Instruction

Professional Development

Learning Environments

© 2007 Partnership for 21st Century Learning (P21)
www.P21.org/Framework

The P21 Rainbow Framework for 21st Century Learning

Note: Although the graphic above represents each element distinctly for descriptive purposes, the Partnership views all the components as fully interconnected in the process of 21st century teaching and learning.

To help practitioners integrate skills into the teaching of key academic subjects, the Partnership for 21st Century Learning (P21) has developed a unified, collective vision for learning known as the Framework for 21st Century Learning. This framework describes the skills, knowledge, and expertise students must master to succeed in work and life; it is a blend of content knowledge, specific skills, expertise, and literacies.

Every system of 21st century skills implementation requires the development of key academic subject knowledge and understanding among all students. Those students who can think critically and communicate effectively must build on a base of key academic subject knowledge.

Within the context of key knowledge instruction, *students must also learn the essential skills for success in today's world, such as critical thinking, problem solving, communication, and collaboration.*

21ˢᵗ Century Student Outcomes

The elements described in this section as "21st century student outcomes" (represented by the rainbow part of the framework above) are the knowledge, skills, and expertise students should master to succeed in work and life in the 21st century.

When a school or district builds on this foundation, combining the entire framework with the necessary support systems—standards, assessments, curriculum and instruction, professional development, and learning environments—students are more engaged in the learning process and graduate better prepared to thrive in today's global economy.

Key Subjects and 21ˢᵗ Century Themes

Mastery of *Key Subjects and 21ˢᵗ Century Themes* is essential for all students in the 21ˢᵗ century. *Key Subjects* include:

- English, reading, or language arts;
- World languages;
- Arts;
- Mathematics;
- Economics;
- Science;
- Geography;
- History; and
- Government and civics.

In addition to these subjects, we believe schools must move not only to include a focus on mastery of key subjects, but also to promote understanding of academic content at much higher levels by weaving interdisciplinary 21ˢᵗ Century Themes, such as the following, into key subjects:

Global Awareness

- Using 21ˢᵗ century skills to understand and address global issues
- Learning from and working collaboratively with individuals representing diverse cultures, religions, and lifestyles in a spirit of mutual respect and open dialogue in personal, work, and community contexts
- Understanding other nations and cultures, including the use of non-English languages

Financial, Economic, Business, and Entrepreneurial Literacy

- Knowing how to make appropriate personal economic choices
- Understanding the role of the economy in society
- Using entrepreneurial skills to enhance workplace productivity and career options

Civic Literacy

- Participating effectively in civic life through knowing how to stay informed and understanding governmental processes

- Exercising the rights and obligations of citizenship at local, state, national, and global levels

- Understanding the local and global implications of civic decisions

Health Literacy

- Obtaining, interpreting, and understanding basic health information and services and using such information and services in ways that enhance health

- Understanding preventive physical and mental health measures, including proper diet, nutrition, exercise, risk avoidance, and stress reduction

- Using available information to make appropriate health-related decisions

- Establishing and monitoring personal and family health goals

- Understanding national and international public health and safety issues

Environmental Literacy

- Demonstrating knowledge and understanding of the environment and the circumstances and conditions affecting it, particularly as relates to air, climate, land, food, energy, water, and eco-systems

- Demonstrating knowledge and understanding of society's impact on the natural world (e.g., population growth, population development, resource consumption rate, etc.)

- Investigating and analyzing environmental issues, and making accurate conclusions about effective solutions

- Taking individual and collective action toward addressing environmental challenges (e.g., participating in global actions and designing solutions that inspire action on environmental issues)

Learning and Innovation Skills

Learning and innovation skills increasingly are being recognized as those that separate students who are prepared for more and more complex life and work environments in the 21st century and those who are not. A focus on creativity, critical thinking, communication,

and collaboration is essential to prepare students for the future:

Creativity and Innovation

Think Creatively

- Use a wide range of idea creation techniques (such as brainstorming).

- Create new and worthwhile ideas (both incremental and radical concepts).

- Elaborate, refine, analyze, and evaluate ideas in order to improve and maximize creative efforts.

Work Creatively with Others

- Develop, implement, and communicate new ideas to others effectively.

- Be open and responsive to new and diverse perspectives; incorporate group input and feedback into the work.

- Demonstrate originality and inventiveness in work and understand the real-world limits to adopting new ideas.

- View failure as an opportunity to learn; understand that creativity and innovation is a long-term,

cyclical process of small successes and frequent mistakes.

Implement Innovations

- Act on creative ideas to make a tangible and useful contribution to the field in which the innovation will occur.

Critical Thinking and Problem Solving

Reason Effectively

- Use various types of reasoning (inductive, deductive, etc.) as appropriate to the situation.

Use Systems Thinking

- Analyze how parts of a whole interact with one another to produce overall outcomes in complex systems.

Make Judgments and Decisions

- Effectively analyze and evaluate evidence, arguments, claims, and beliefs.

- Analyze and evaluate major alternative points of view.

- Synthesize and make connections between information and arguments.

- Interpret information and draw conclusions based on the best analysis.
- Reflect critically on learning experiences and processes.

Solve Problems

- Solve different kinds of nonfamiliar problems in both conventional and innovative ways.
- Identify and ask significant questions that clarify various points of view and lead to better solutions.

Communication and Collaboration

Communicate Clearly

- Articulate thoughts and ideas effectively using oral, written, and nonverbal communication skills in a variety of forms and contexts.
- Listen effectively to decipher meaning, including knowledge, values, attitudes, and intentions.
- Use communication for a range of purposes (e.g., to inform, instruct, motivate, and persuade).
- Utilize multiple media and technologies, and know how to judge their effectiveness a priori as well as assess their impact.
- Communicate effectively in diverse environments (including multilingual).

Collaborate with Others

- Demonstrate ability to work effectively and respectfully with diverse teams.
- Exercise flexibility and willingness to be helpful in making necessary compromises to accomplish a common goal.
- Assume shared responsibility for collaborative work, and value the individual contributions made by each team member.

Information, Media, and Technology Skills

People in the 21st century live in a technology- and media-driven environment, marked by various characteristics, including (1) access to an abundance of information, (2) rapid changes in technology tools, and (3) the ability to collaborate and make individual contributions on an unprecedented scale. Effective citizens and workers of the 21st century must be able to exhibit a range of functional and critical thinking skills related to information, media, and technology.

Information Literacy

Access and Evaluate Information

- Access information efficiently (time) and effectively (appropriate sources).
- Evaluate information critically and competently.

Use and Manage Information

- Use information accurately and creatively for the issue or problem at hand.

- Manage the flow of information from a wide variety of sources.

- Apply a fundamental understanding of the ethical/legal issues surrounding the access and use of information.

Media Literacy

Analyze Media

- Understand both how and why media messages are constructed, and for what purposes.

- Examine how individuals interpret messages differently, how values and points of view are included or excluded, and how media can influence beliefs and behaviors.

- Apply a fundamental understanding of the ethical/legal issues surrounding the access and use of media.

Create Media Products

- Understand and utilize the most appropriate media creation tools, characteristics, and conventions.

- Understand and effectively utilize the most appropriate expressions and interpretations in diverse, multicultural environments.

ICT (Information, Communications, and Technology) Literacy

Apply Technology Effectively

- Use technology as a tool to research, organize, evaluate, and communicate information.

- Use digital technologies (computers, PDAs, media players, GPS, etc.), communication/networking tools, and social networks appropriately to access, manage, integrate, evaluate, and create information to successfully function in a knowledge economy.

- Apply a fundamental understanding of the ethical/legal issues surrounding the access and use of information technologies.

Life and Career Skills

Today's life and work environments require far more than thinking skills and content knowledge. The ability to navigate the complex life and work environments in the globally competitive information age requires students to pay rigorous attention to developing adequate life and career skills.

Flexibility and Adaptability

Adapt to Change

- Adapt to varied roles, jobs, responsibilities, schedules, and contexts.
- Work effectively in a climate of ambiguity and changing priorities.

Be Flexible

- Incorporate feedback effectively.
- Deal positively with praise, setbacks, and criticism.
- Understand, negotiate, and balance diverse views and beliefs to reach workable solutions, particularly in multicultural environments.

Initiative and Self-Direction

Manage Goals and Time

- Set goals with tangible and intangible success criteria.
- Balance tactical (short-term) and strategic (long-term) goals.
- Utilize time and manage workload efficiently.

Work Independently

- Monitor, define, prioritize, and complete tasks without direct oversight.

Be Self-Directed Learners

- Go beyond basic mastery of skills and/or curriculum to explore and expand students' own learning and opportunities to gain expertise.
- Demonstrate initiative to advance skill levels toward a professional level.
- Demonstrate commitment to learning as a lifelong process.
- Reflect critically on past experiences in order to inform future progress.

Social and Cross-Cultural Skills

Interact Effectively with Others

- Know when it is appropriate to listen and when to speak.
- Conduct themselves in a respectable, professional manner.

Work Effectively in Diverse Teams

- Respect cultural differences and work effectively with people from a range of social and cultural backgrounds.
- Respond open-mindedly to different ideas and values.
- Leverage social and cultural differences to create new ideas and increase both innovation and quality of work.

Productivity and Accountability

Manage Projects

- Set and meet goals, even in the face of obstacles and competing pressures.
- Prioritize, plan, and manage work to achieve the intended result.

Produce Results

- Demonstrate additional attributes associated with producing high-quality products, including the abilities to:
  - ○ Work positively and ethically;
  - ○ Manage time and projects effectively;

- ○ Multitask;
- ○ Participate actively, as well as be reliable and punctual;
- ○ Present oneself professionally and with proper etiquette;
- ○ Collaborate and cooperate effectively with teams;
- ○ Respect and appreciate team diversity; and
- ○ Be accountable for results.

Leadership and Responsibility

Guide and Lead Others

- Use interpersonal and problem-solving skills to influence and guide others toward a goal.
- Leverage strengths of others to accomplish a common goal.
- Inspire others to reach their very best via example and selflessness.
- Demonstrate integrity and ethical behavior in using influence and power.

Be Responsible to Others

- Act responsibly with the interests of the larger community in mind.

Project Learning Resources

Project Method Frameworks Comparisons

Here is a chart showing the similarities, differences and alignments between project method frameworks (indicated by different colored columns) for learning projects, professional project management, project based learning, design thinking, engineering design, scientific inquiry, and debate and expression projects:

Learning Projects	Project Management	Project Based Learning	Design Thinking	Engineering Design	Scientific Inquiry	Debate Projects	Expression Projects
Define	Initiating	Launch the project	Empathize and Define	Identify the Problem and Learn the Specifications	Pose a Question	Choose an Issue	Reflect on a personal perspective you'd like to communicate to others
Plan	Planning	Build skills to address the driving question	Ideate	Brainstorm Solutions and Design It	Research the Question and Formulate a Hypothesis	Research the issue and form an evidence-based position	Choose a medium of expression; design, plan and create a rough prototype
Do	Executing & Controlling/ Monitoring	Develop and critique products & answers	Prototype	Build It, Test, Improve and Redesign	Test the Hypothesis by Experiments	Present and logically argue its strengths and limits	Test the prototype on others, get feedback, and create or perform the work
Review	Closing	Present products and answers	Test (Refine Prototype and Re-Test until satisfied)	Share It	Analyze and Present the Results	Assess the persuasive impact on others	Evaluate your feelings & gauge others' reactions to the work

Project Learning Resources

Educational Research on Project Learning

Evidence That Project Learning Works

(Note: This section is adapted from *21st Century Skills: Learning for Life in Our Times* by Trilling and Fadel.)

There is a strong and growing body of research evidence that learning through a project approach, as detailed in this guide, can help students:

- Learn more deeply when they apply their knowledge to real-world problems and take part in projects that require sustained engagement and collaboration;

- Achieve higher levels of academic achievement and personal development with active and collaborative learning practices that can have more impact on student performance than a student's background or prior achievement; and

- Become more successful in learning when they are taught *how* to learn as well as *what* to learn, as a project approach allows.

These summary conclusions are based on a thorough review of the 50-plus-year research base on inquiry, design, and collaborative approaches to learning by noted Stanford University education researcher, professor, and policy advisor Linda Darling-Hammond and her colleagues.

Professor Darling-Hammond and her colleagues reviewed the accumulated research on three learning approaches based on inquiry and design methods of teaching and learning: collaborative small-group learning, project learning methods, problem-based learning, and design-based project learning and innovation.

The following are the summary findings from their analyses of the research base for each of these learning methods, all of which are used in learning projects.

Collaborative Small-Group Learning

Students working in small teams on collective tasks have been the subject of hundreds of educational studies.

All the research arrives at the same conclusion: There are significant benefits for students who work together on learning activities compared to students who work alone. These benefits include:

- Greater individual and collective knowledge growth,

- Better confidence and motivation levels, and

- Improved social interactions and feelings toward other students.

In a comparison of four types of problems presented to both individuals and cooperative teams, researchers found that teams outperform individuals on all problem types and across all ages. In addition, individuals who work in groups do better on individual assessments as well.

Project Learning Methods

Project learning involves completing complex tasks that result in a realistic product, event, or presentation to an audience.

Well-designed, effective project learning has five key characteristics:

1. Project outcomes are tied to curriculum and learning goals.

2. Driving questions and problems lead students to the central concepts or principles of the topic or subject area.

3. Student investigations and research involve inquiry, problem solving, and knowledge building.

4. Students are responsible for designing and managing much of their own learning.

5. Projects are based on authentic, real-world problems and questions that students care about.

Research on learning projects having these qualities found that student gains in factual learning were equal to or better than those using more traditional classroom instructional methods. But when studies took the time to measure gains in other skills, in particular the higher-order, 21st century skills, the learning gains were significantly higher than with traditional methods.

An ambitious three-year longitudinal study of students in two schools in England, matched for similar income and student achievement levels, found that significantly more students passed the National Exams in the school that used project approaches to learning math than in the school that used more traditional textbook and work-sheet approaches. Project learning students also developed more flexible and useful math knowledge than their textbook-oriented counterparts.

A type of project learning, problem-based learning involves projects focused on solving complex, real-world problems using a case study approach. Students work in small groups to investigate, research, and create solutions to problems that could have multiple solutions and methods for reaching them.

Much of the research comes from medical education, where medical students are challenged to provide the proper diagnosis, tests, and treatment for a simulated patient's case (based on real patient histories). This case method has also been used effectively in law and business education, as well as other professional learning settings, including teacher education.

Studies and meta-studies of problem-based learning and research show that, similar to the findings from project learning research, for factual learning, problem-based methods are equal to or better than traditional instruction. But problem-based methods far outshine traditional methods in developing 21st century skills such as flexible problem solving and applying knowledge to real-world situations, as well as critical thinking skills such as generating testable hypotheses and communicating more coherent explanations.

The Cognition and Technology Group at Vanderbilt University (CTGV) studied problem approaches to learning for over a decade. In one study of more than 700 students from 11 school districts engaged in solving problems from CTGV's popular *Jasper Woodbury* series of video-based challenges, students experienced much larger gains than those in the comparison group for all five of the areas measured:

- Understanding math concepts,
- Doing word problems,
- Planning approaches to problem solving,
- Having positive attitudes toward math, and
- Providing feedback to teachers.

Design-Based Project Learning and Innovation

Design-based learning approaches can be found across many subject disciplines, including science, art, technology, engineering, and architecture. The international FIRST Robotics competition is an example of highly engaging, design-oriented learning where student teams design, build, and guide their robots in a competitive series of sports-like physical challenges.

In another design-based project example, a five-week project that used the design of a playground structure to present basic principles of geometry, the CTGV found that 5th-grade students of all ability levels made significant

gains in their measurement and scaling skills, scoring well on standard tests of geometric concepts. Thirty-one of the 37 playground designs submitted by students were judged accurate enough to be built—a very high rate of achievement.

Though there are increasing demands for skills in science, technology, engineering, and math, the so-called STEM skills, the demands for creativity, invention, and innovation are growing across all fields of study and work. The arts have been a traditional source for developing creativity and innovation. Integrating the arts in STEM is an important education goal for the 21st century.

How do we best prepare our students for a future of work that does not yet exist, careers that have not been invented, an economy that prizes things not yet created, and that integrates knowledge, skills, character qualities and learning how to learn into the educational plans for every child?

Learning projects anchored in the phases of the project cycle—Define, Plan, Do, and Review—can deeply engage students in learning activities that build creative skills. With some slight additions and modifications to the phases of the project cycle, the odds of a project team coming up with innovative ideas and solutions can go way up. Here

are some suggestions as to how to increase innovation and creativity throughout the project cycle:

- *Define (Initiating)*—Focus on real-world problems or processes whose solutions will make things easier, better, faster, less expensive, more effective, or more enjoyable. A "How might we . . ." question followed by the definition of the problem—for example, How might we use the sun's energy to inexpensively provide a nighttime flashlight for use in homes in rural areas without electricity?—is key to getting a design project off to a good start.

- *Plan (Planning)*—Take the time to *understand* the users, clients, technology, market or field, and constraints on the problem you're tackling. Closely and frequently observe how real people in real-life situations deal with the problem or condition at hand and create detailed profiles of typical people and their experiences with the issue.

For both the Define and Plan phases of a project a diverse project team is important to the innovation process—the more diversity, the better the chance of coming up with fresh, out-of-the-box solutions.

- *Do (Executing & Monitoring/Controlling)*—Using a wide variety of visualizing and brainstorming

techniques, come up with a wealth of possible design solutions and sort through the positives and negatives of each one. Choose the most promising design and create a prototype of it. Test it with a variety of real people in real problem situations and keep careful records of the results.

- *Review (Closing)*—Evaluate and refine a series of prototypes in quick iterations, each time eliminating difficulties or confusion, enhancing the benefits, making better design trade-offs, and improving the overall solution.

The *Do* and *Review* phases are repeated often in this phase of the innovation-enhanced version of the design project cycle, bouncing back and forth between the two,

with lessons learned from the *Review* evaluations immediately applied to the next *Do* round of creating an improved prototype.

Finally, the innovation is implemented, with user feedback and new ideas for improvements eventually prompting a brand-new trip through the project cycle and another quest for useful innovation.

This design-for-innovation project cycle can be seen as a powerful design approach to learning. In fact, the design process itself is a powerful learning process that produces innovative results, applies and builds the project team's creative skills, and develops a deep understanding of the problem area and its possible solutions.

PMIEF Resources

Get Inspired Video Collection

This video collection shares stories of global project management programs, highlighting learning projects and project management practices involving teachers, students, youth nonprofits programs, and project managers from around the world.

https://pmief.org/library/impact-stories-and-videos

21st Century Skills Map™

The 21st Century Skills Map provides a crosswalk between project management skills, 21st century skills and career pathways. The Skills Map shows which 21st Century Skills are developed in each of the four stages of a learning project.

https://pmief.org/library/resources/21st-century-skills-map

Project Management Toolkit for Teachers™

The Project Management Toolkit for Teachers™ provides a modular, user-friendly resource that teachers can use to help prepare youth aged 12–18 to be college and career ready through engaging learning projects. The toolkit has two versions, a general PBL learning projects version and a standard project management terminology version.

https://pmief.org/library/resources/project-management-toolkit-for-teachers

Project Management Resource for Primary Schools™

Based on *Projects From the Future: Primary Schools*, this guide offers educators a wealth of exemplary project practices specially tailored to the needs of young project learners.

https://pmief.org/library/resources/projects-from-the-future-kit-for-primary-school

Project Management for Career and Technical Education™

Project Management for Career & Technical Education offers project management-rich curricula for secondary school business, finance and marketing teachers who would like to integrate project management into their coursework.

https://pmief.org/library/resources/project-management-for-career-and-technical-education

Digital Teacher Badging/Micro-certification Toolkit

PMIEF badges/micro-credentials allow teachers to provide verifiable evidence of their ability to integrate project management into classroom instruction for enhanced learning and outcomes. Six badges/micro-certifications are available and teachers can do one or all six, some states provide CEUs for teachers who earn the badges/micro-certifications.

https://pmief.org/library/resources/digital-teacher-badging-toolkit

Digital Student Badging Toolkit

PMIEF offers a Project Management Fundamentals digital badge for students aged 12–19 years who have developed project management skills and knowledge in school or as part of an extracurricular activity.

https://pmief.org/library/resources/digital-student-badging-toolkit

Practice Guide for School Teachers

Being able to assess and measure effectiveness and progress are important components for any program. This assessment tool, can be used to measure progress on any youth-oriented project management program.

https://pmief.org/library/resources/project-management-kit-for-primary-school-practice-guide

Managing Life's Projects™

Managing Life's Projects is a versatile resource for providing training in the fundamentals of project management to a variety of audiences.

https://pmief.org/library/resources/managing-lifes-projects

Project Management Skills for Life®

Project Management Skills for Life® is a guide that provides an introduction to the basics of project management as well

as tools and techniques to help develop skills to become a proficient project manager leading successful projects

https://pmief.org/library/resources/project-management-skills-for-life

Careers in Project Management™

Why consider a career in project management? In this booklet you will find salary information, career pathways and additional information about a career in project management.

https://pmief.org/library/resources/careers-in-project-management

PBL Resources

PBL for 21st Century Success by Suzie Boss, the National Faculty, and BIE

Part of Buck Institute for Education's (BIE) PBL Toolkit Series this guide connects PBL practices and learning the 4C 21st century skills.

https://shop.bie.org/pbl-for-21st-century-success-p37.aspx

PBL Starter Kit by John Larmer, David Ross, and John Mergendoller

Part of BIE's PBL Toolkit Series this guide helps middle and high school teachers get started with learning projects.

https:\\bie.org

PBL in the Elementary Grades by Sara Hallermann, John Larmer, and John Mergendoller

Part of BIE's Toolkit Series this guide gives step-by-step help and tips for doing learning projects in grades K–5.

https:\\bie.org

Setting the Standard for Project Based Learning by John Larmer, John Mergendoller, and Suzie Boss

Part of BIE's efforts to establish a "Gold Standard" for PBL, this guide offers attributes and practices of exemplary PBL learning projects for both teachers and students.

https:\\bie.org

Reinventing Project-Based Learning, 2nd Ed. by Suzie Boss and Jane Krauss

An International Society for Technology in Education (ISTE) guide with a focus on powering up PBL with technology tools.

https://www.iste.org/resources/product?id=3496&format=Book&name=Reinventing+Project-Based+Learning%2c+2nd+Edition

Young Reader Resources

The Project Kids Adventures Series by Gary Nelson

1. The Ultimate Tree House Project
2. The Scariest Haunted House Project – Ever
3. The Amazing Science Fair Project
4. The Valentine's Day Project Disaster
5. The Easter Bully Transformation Project

An adventure series that helps students learn how and how not to do fun projects.

https://pmief.org/library/resources/project-management-fiction-books-for-youth-ages-10-12

Basic Professional Project Management Resources

Fundamentals of Project Management, 5th Ed. by Joseph Heagney

A best-selling American Management Association publication that clearly presents the basics of project management principles and practices.

https://www.amazon.com/Fundamentals-Project-Management-Joseph-Heagney/dp/0814437362

Project Management for Dummies, 4th Ed. by Stanley Portney, PMP

A graphic guide to the essential elements of basic project management methods.

Basic Professional Agile Project Management Resources

A graphic guide to the essential elements of basic agile project management methods.

https://www.amazon.com/Agile-Project-Management-Dummies-Layton/dp/1118026241/

PMIEF Resources

Project Management Kit: A Practical Guide for Tutors and Mentors®

The Practical Guide for Tutors is designed to provide guidance for PMs and others who are tutoring/mentoring teachers to help them learn how to effectively deliver project management experiences in their classrooms.

https://pmief.org/library/resources/project-management-kit-for-primary-school-practice-guide-for-tutors

PMI Resources

A Guide to the Project Management Body of Knowledge (PMBOK® Guide), 5th Ed.

The "Bible" of the project management profession offering a global ANSI standard version for project management professionals.

https://www.pmi.org

Life, Learning, and Professional Project Glossary

Life, Learning and Professional Project Glossary

The following chart alphabetically lists 50 of the most common professional project management terms and their definitions (blue columns three and four), with their related life skills project terms (yellow column one) and learning project terms (green column two) where there are appropriate substitutes:

Life Skills Project Terms	Learning Project Terms	Career/Professional Project Terms	Career/Professional Project Terms Definitions
Activity	Activity	Activity	A distinct, scheduled portion of work performed during the course of a project.
Given	Assumption	Assumption	A factor in the planning process that is considered to be true, real or certain, without proof or demonstration.
Project Examples	Model Learning Projects	Baseline	The approved version of a work product that can be changed only through formal change control procedures and is used as a basis for comparison.
	Work Plan Estimates	Bottom-up Estimating	A method of estimating project duration or cost by aggregating the estimates of the lower-level components of the work breakdown structure.
Change	Change Request	Change Request	A formal proposal to modify any document, deliverable, or baseline.
Can't Do	Limit	Constraint	A limiting factor that affects the execution of a project, program, portfolio, or process.

(continued)

Life Skills Project Terms	Learning Project Terms	Career/Professional Project Terms	Career/Professional Project Terms Definitions
Step Change	Work Plan Change	Corrective Action	An intentional activity that realigns the performance of the project work with the project management plan.
Get Help		Crashing	A technique used to shorten the schedule duration for the least incremental cost by adding resources. See also Fast Tracking.
	Cushion	Critical Chain Method	A schedule method that allows the project team to place buffers on any project schedule path to account for limited resources and project uncertainties.
		Critical Path Method	A method used to estimate the minimum project duration and determine the amount of scheduling flexibility on the logical network paths within the schedule model.
Step Planning	Task Planning	Decomposition	A technique used for dividing and sub-dividing the project scope and project deliverables into smaller, more manageable parts.
Fix	Result Improvement	Defect Repair	An intentional activity to modify a non-conforming product or product component.
Step Done	Completed Result	Deliverable	Any unique and verifiable product, result, or capability to perform a service that must be produced to complete a process, phase, or project.
Work	Work Plan Estimate	Effort	The number of labor units required to complete a schedule activity or work break-down structure component, often expressed in hours, days or weeks.
Parallel Steps	Parallel Work	Fast Tracking	A schedule compression technique in which activities or phases normally done in sequence are performed in parallel for at least a portion of their duration.
Checklist	Gantt Chart	Gantt Chart	A bar chart of schedule information where activities are listed on the vertical axis, dates are shown on the horizontal axis, and activity durations are shown as horizontal bars placed according to start and finish dates.
Team	Team Agreement	Human Resource Plan	A component of the project or program management plan that describes how the roles and responsibilities, reporting relationships and staff management will be addressed and structured.
Wait	Delay	Lag	The amount of time whereby a successor activity must be delayed with respect to a predecessor activity.
Lessons	Project Methods Evaluation	Lessons Learned	The knowledge gained during a project which shows how project events were addressed or should be addressed in the future with the purpose of improving future performance.

(continued)

Life Skills Project Terms	Learning Project Terms	Career/Professional Project Terms	Career/Professional Project Terms Definitions
Step Completed	Milestone	Milestone	A significant point or event in a project, program or portfolio.
Break	Opportunity	Opportunity	A risk that would have a positive effect on one or more project objectives.
Steps Completed	Work Completed	Percent Complete	An estimate expressed as a percent of the amount of work that has been completed on an activity or a work breakdown structure component.
	Learning Project Portfolio	Portfolio	Projects, programs, subportfolios, and operations managed as a group to achieve strategic objectives.
		Probability and Impact Matrix	A grid for mapping the probability of each risk occurrence and its impact on project objectives if that risk occurs.
		Preventive Action	An intentional activity that ensures the future performance of the project work is aligned with the project management plan.
	Learning Program, Curriculum	Program	A group of related projects, subprograms and program activities managed in a coordinated way to obtain benefits not available from managing them individually.
	Learning Program, Curriculum Plan	Program Management	The application of knowledge, skills, tools, and techniques to a program to meet the program requirements and to obtain benefits and control not available by managing projects individually.
	Learning	Progressive Elaboration	The iterative process of increasing the level of detail in a project management plan as greater amounts of information and more accurate estimates become available.
Project	Project	Project	A temporary endeavor undertaken to create a unique product, service, or result.
Schedule	Project Calendar	Project Calendar	A calendar that identifies working days and shifts that are available for scheduled activities.
	Project	Project	
Plan	Project Portfolio (Proj. Definition, Team Agreement & Work Plan)	Project Charter	A document issued by the project initiator or sponsor that formally authorizes the existence of a project and provides the project manager with the authority to apply organizational resources to project activities.
Project Cycle	Project Cycle	Project Life Cycle	The series of phases that a project passes through from its initiation to its closure.
Project Steps	Project Mgmt. & Leadership	Project Management	The application of knowledge, skills, tools, and techniques to project activities to meet the project requirements.

(continued)

Life Skills Project Terms	Learning Project Terms	Career/Professional Project Terms	Career/Professional Project Terms Definitions
Project Organizer	Project Manager	Project Manager	The person assigned by the performing organization to lead the team that is responsible for achieving the project objectives.
Project Step	Project Phase	Project Phase	A collection of logically related project activities that culminates in the completion of one or more deliverables.
Checklist	Work Plan	Project Schedule	An output of a schedule model that presents linked activities with planned dates, durations, milestones, and resources.
	Mind Map	Project Schedule Network Diagram	A graphical representation of the logical relationships among the project schedule activities.
Size of Project	Project Definition	Project Scope	The work performed to deliver a product, service, or result with the specified features and functions.
Need	Requirement	Requirement	A condition or capability that must be present in a product, service, or result to satisfy a contract or other formally imposed specification.
	Risk	Risk	An uncertain event or condition that, if it occurs, has a positive or negative effect on one or more project objectives.
		Rolling Wave Planning	An iterative planning technique in which the work to be accomplished in the near term is planned in detail, while the work in the future is planned at a higher level.
Checklist	Work Plan	Schedule Baseline	The approved version of a schedule model that can be changed only through formal change control procedures and is used as a basis for comparison to actual results.
Hurry	Rush	Schedule Compression	A technique used to shorten the schedule duration without reducing the project scope.
Extra Work	Project Additions	Scope Creep	The uncontrolled expansion to product or project scope without adjustments to time, cost and resources.
Project Organizer	Champion	Sponsor	A person or group who provides resources and support for the project, program, or portfolio, and is accountable for enabling success.

(continued)